Speech Writing and Delivery for Public Relations

Colleen McMahon
Gonzaga University

Ron Prindle
Gonzaga University

Kendall Hunt
publishing company

Cover image © Shutterstock, Inc.

www.kendallhunt.com
Send all inquiries to:
4050 Westmark Drive
Dubuque, IA 52004-1840

Copyright © 2015 by Kendall Hunt Publishing Company

ISBN 978-1-4652-6654-5

Printed in the United States of America

Contents

About the Authors

Colleen McMahon, MA, is an Associate Professor of Public Relations in the Integrated Media Department at Gonzaga University. She teaches public relations speech writing and delivery and has taught advanced public speaking for over 30 years. She has published books on Interpersonal Communication and Public Speaking, and has vast experience as a communication trainer and consultant. She has also served as Associate Dean for the College of Arts and Sciences at Gonzaga.

Ron Prindle, Ph.D., is an Assistant Professor of Public Relations in the Integrated Media Department at Gonzaga University. He teaches public relations and public speaking courses and served for five years as the Public Relations Program Director. Prior to entering academia, Dr. Prindle worked for over 30 years in a variety of military, public sector and private sector organizations.

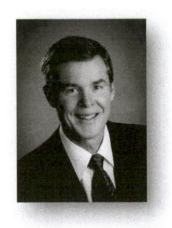

Preface

The need is greater than ever for organizations to have a strong public relations team that can project the corporate image, respond to crises, speak on behalf of the organization and, above all, protect and promote the brand. While there has been an exponential growth in the popularity and use of social media platforms as channels of communication to accomplish these requirements, audiences and publics still demand face-to-face interaction with the organization. Public speaking is a key component of this face-to-face communication with an organization's publics.

We have learned from both entry-level and experienced public relations practitioners that their undergraduate college course work did not include public speaking at all or, in some cases, included only a basic communication course. In most cases, they have not been trained at a more *advanced* level to write and deliver the kinds of presentations that public relations professionals routinely make. Furthermore, they may have little or no experience in writing public relations presentations for *others* to deliver (CEOs, politicians, corporate spokespersons, etc.) or in executive coaching for those who are actually delivering the presentation.

Accordingly, this book was written to fill what we perceive to be a void in advanced public relations public speaking training and experience. This book was written for the reader who wants to know more about public speaking in a public relations context. What distinguishes this book from traditional college public speaking textbooks is the emphasis on specific public relations examples and exercises designed to give the reader practical knowledge and experience.

The reader will receive exposure, training, and the practice in writing for others and giving the kinds of speeches and public in-person presentations at which public relations professionals must excel. Readers will learn skills that give their speech design, writing and delivery a polished edge. The reader will also learn techniques of effective evaluation. The reader will develop the knowledge and skills to confidently and effectively talk to the media, as well as demonstrate understanding of coaching and stagecraft considerations for corporate spokespersons. This book recognizes that Public Relations students and practitioners wish to explore speech writing, speaking and analytical opportunities to gain a higher level of expertise in verbally presenting the self in a variety of public relations contexts.

The journey in writing this book was entirely collaborative. We drew from decades of organizational experience and years of teaching public speaking and public relations courses. The actual writing of the content of the book came about rather quickly, because in a sense, we have been writing this book for years, but never knew it.

A number of people have contributed to the completion of this book. We give special thanks to Associate Professor Susan English for her copyediting of the manuscript, professional advice and support; to Sandy Hank for formatting finalization; and, our publishing team of Scott Wallace and Brenda Rolwes for enthusiastically embracing our idea for the book and shepherding us through the publication process. We are also grateful to two of our students, Shaniqua Nilles and Kathleen Miyakado, for the writing samples they contributed.

Chapter 1

Contemporary Public Speaking

© Rawpixel/Shutterstock.com

Objectives

At the completion of this chapter you should be able to:

- ✓ Utilize the "Energizer Effect" to alleviate speaker anxiety.

- ✓ Outline and organize a presentation.

- ✓ Differentiate between a thesis and a specific purpose.

- ✓ Maintain credibility by adhering to high ethical standards.

Studies show that the higher you climb the corporate ladder, the more opportunities you will have to give presentations. Since most people don't aspire to stay at the bottom rung, the more you can learn about writing and delivering effective presentations, the more successful you will be. Public speaking is one of the most important skills you can acquire, whether you are a student, a corporate executive, or public relations professional. This chapter will provide you with a refresher and overview of contemporary public speaking if you have never taken a public speaking course, or it has been a while since doing so. By the time you finish reading this chapter you will know how to overcome the fear of speaking in front of an audience, know how to outline and organize a presentation, and maintain credibility by adhering to high ethical standards.

DEALING WITH SPEECH ANXIETY

You've been asked to make a presentation—now what?

"What if I am nervous?" You are not alone. Most people, even the most seasoned speakers and celebrities, admit that they experience some anxiety before making a presentation. You've probably also heard that what people fear the most is speaking before a group, according to the *Book of Lists*. Public speaking is feared more than even snakes or death. Now that doesn't

necessarily mean that people would rather die than give a speech, but it does point out that the fear of public speaking is a common phenomenon. "The fear of public speaking can take two forms: psychological and physiological."* Let's first look at the psychological cause. According to "Alfred Adler's theory of the 'inferiority complex,' most humans at one time or another believe they are inferior. This is a result of our natural desire to

© Danomyte/Shutterstock.com

3

be loved and approved. A certain amount of that desire is healthy. But you can set yourself up for failure when you want too much approval. If you analyze why people feel a great fear of public speaking, it usually boils down to an apprehension about making a fool of themselves. If you believe a situation will make you look foolish, you are most likely going to avoid it."* For example, some of you will never step foot on a dance floor for fear of having two left feet. Others of us would never sing karaoke because we might sing off key. While some anxiety is in our heads, as discussed above, other anxiety is manifested physically.

Let's now look at the physiological causes. Our bodies react physically to stressful situations in a variety of ways. "Often this reaction happens because of a perceived lack of control."* For example, have you ever driven on ice? No matter what you try to do, such as pumping your brakes or attempting to steer in a different direction, the car seems to have a mind of its own. As a result, our stress mechanism kicks in and we may start shaking, we may perspire, break out in hives, or experience some other unpleasant physiological reaction. These physical – or stress – reactions are often beyond our control.

"Hans Seyle, a pioneer in the study of stress, divides the stress reaction into two categories: negative and positive. On one hand, stress can wear an anxious public speaker down if he or she feels feel panicky for a long time. This is known as negative stress. However, stress can also help an anxious public speaker focus and be more prepared. This is known as positive stress."* For example, imagine you are getting ready to take a vacation. As you prepare for the trip, you have a list of things to do so you don't forget anything. You double check that you have everything packed, that you have your airline boarding pass ready, etc. You are excited about the trip and you make sure you have everything you need to have fun. Your heart may race a little as you head to the airport, but this is the kind of positive stress that is in effect excitement and anticipation.

Careful Preparation

Most of the time speakers fear that they may lose their place, they may forget some of their material, that their visual aids may not function properly, or they may worry that their presentation will be boring. While these fears can produce anxiety, this pre-speech nervousness can also work in your favor. There is good news! "One of the most comforting phenomena for speakers is the 'Energizer Effect.' The Energizer Effect occurs when three elements combine during a speech: a

> **Perception is Reality**
>
> If you see the speech as intimidating and unpleasant, stress can be negative. On the other hand, if you're prepared and have a desire to share your ideas with an audience, those perceptions can be quite positive.

nervous speaker, an audience, and the speaker has carefully prepared. Those three factors blend to make the material more vivid in the speaker's mind."* So, when the speaker knows her material well and has carefully rehearsed, even though she experiences a certain amount of anxiety when getting up in front of a group, the speaker recalls her material more clearly and she comes across as energetic and excited.

Conversely, if the speaker is unprepared, this lack of preparation will amplify those feelings of anxiety, leading to an ineffective presentation. If you're still not convinced that the Energizer Effect works, then think about a time when you studied really hard before an exam. You spent hours

© Arek_malang/Shutterstock.com

going over the material and now it is time to put the pen to paper. The instructor hands you the essay exam. You see the question and can't wait to start writing. Your pen can't keep up with your thoughts. You know this stuff! That's because you studied the material carefully. Your careful preparation made the material that you studied more vivid in your mind. The same can happen with careful speech preparation.

Preparation builds confidence. Learn as much as you can about your audience and the setting (we will talk more about audience analysis in Chapter 3). Start working on your presentation early so you can have your ideas floating around in your mind as you take a walk or drive in your car. Practice your delivery under conditions that are as similar as possible to the actual speaking situation. If you know you are going to be presenting in a large room, try to get in a practice run with the audiovisual equipment prior to the speaking day. Try your material out on a family member or friend to get feedback on clarity and understanding. Get your presentation down to a key-word outline so you are not tempted to read your speech word for word. Anxiety is usually the highest at the beginning, so make sure your opener is almost committed to memory.

Practice positive thinking both before and during your presentation. Replace negative thoughts with positive ones. Am I nervous? No. Excited? Yes! You have carefully prepared and now you are ready. Hopefully you have visited the room where you are presenting in advance and you can visualize yourself in the setting. Imagine yourself delivering a dynamic presentation and picture the audience nodding with approval and applauding at the end. Practice deep breathing; breathe in through the nose and out through the mouth. This practice calms the entire body and instead of focusing on your fears, you are focusing on your breathing. Exercising an hour or two before your presentation can release endorphins and help you focus on feeling good about what lies ahead.

When it is time for you to speak, walk up to the front of the room with your head held high and act confident. You have done your preparation and it is time to shine. Look around the room, smile, and make eye contact. See who smiles back and make sure you look at them during your speech. If you feel uncomfortable smiling, give them an eyebrow flash – raise your eyebrows. It makes you look relaxed. If nerves kick in, use your notes as much as you need during your introduction to get over the hurdle. That will help build some confidence as you speak your first couple of sentences. Most importantly, never let them see you sweat; in other words, don't admit that you are nervous. Often, the audience can't tell unless you tell them. You look better than you may actually feel. Again, that's that Energizer Effect. Lastly, make direct eye contact. Your audience expects it, and when you avoid making eye contact you can actually increase your anxiety.

We cannot stress enough that preparation is key to reducing speech anxiety! You will never completely eliminate anxiety, or "butterflies," before and during a public presentation. You can, however, considerably reduce and use to your benefit public speaking apprehension. While most people will experience at least some butterflies when facing a public speaking opportunity, the goal is to get those butterflies to fly in formation!

Now that we've learned how to manage our anxiety through careful preparation, let's get to work on creating the speech!

SPEECH ORGANIZATION

Specific Purpose and Thesis

Before you write your speech, you must determine the purpose of your presentation and your key points. A good starting point is to define your *specific purpose*. A specific purpose states your intent. For example, as your local food bank's public relations spokesperson, your purpose might be: "To educate local school districts about the weekend backpack program the food bank provides for children who rely on free lunch programs." Your goal, in this instance, is to educate, or perhaps promote goodwill. Once you have defined your purpose, you need to define your *thesis*. What is your main point, bottom line, or central idea of your presentation? Your thesis should be a one-sentence, summary statement that clearly articulates your main point. Using the food bank example again, your thesis statement would be: "The weekend backpack program provided by the food bank allows low-income children who rely on free school lunches to take home a backpack full of nutritious, non-perishable food to enjoy over the weekend."

The Speech Outline

Once you have identified your purpose and thesis, you can begin to write the body of your speech. If you try to write word-for-word in manuscript form, it will take a very long time to put your thoughts together. Instead, creating an outline is the best way to build your ideas. A

© AnaWhite/Shutterstock.com

well- developed outline will include an introduction, a body, and a conclusion. We advocate the use of a conventional three-level, full-sentence outline that includes Roman numerals and alternating letters and numbers. The length of the outline will be determined by the length of time allotted for the presentation. Your speech outline is a roadmap for both you as speaker, and the audience as your listener. "One rule of thumb in speechwriting is that the more you know about your topic, the less detail will be needed in your outline. Conversely, the less you know about your topic, the more detail will be required in your outline."* You probably have varied experiences with creating outlines for speeches or other purposes; but, rest assured, a well-organized outline will give you more confidence and a better command of your material. A sample outline is provided at the end of this chapter.

The Body

Although it may seem logical to write the *introduction* first, speechwriting best practices dictate that we develop the *body* first and then create the *introduction* and *conclusion*. After all, how can you write your introduction when you haven't even figured out what you are introducing? Many people spend far too much time trying to write the introduction to their speech before they write the body. This is a costly mistake.

The body of the speech builds on your thesis statement. In other words, your main points in the body should all connect back to the thesis. For comprehension, an audience can really only retain a limited number of main points. Shoot for no more than three to five, depending on the length of the speech. Main points should be supported with sub-points. A main point should not stand alone.

Main points should follow a coherent method of organization that is appropriate to your purpose, i.e., informing or persuading. For an informational speech, organize your points chronologically or categorically. For example, referring back to the earlier food bank backpack example, you can describe chronologically the steps the food bank takes in putting together the individual backpacks before they are distributed to students.

© Lorelyn Medina/Shutterstock.com

In a persuasive presentation, your main points should argue logically in support of your thesis statement. Using the food bank backpack program example, imagine a speaker who is speaking to an audience of potential donors. Using the premise that children who do not eat well do not perform well in school, the speaker tells the audience that these same children who rely on free lunches during the week do not have access to nutritious food over the weekend, thereby necessitating support for the backpack program.

Within the body of the speech you also want to provide transitions between the main points of the speech. These transitional words or phrases keep listeners moving along with the speaker so they know you are done talking about one point and moving on to the next. Another useful tool is providing periodic internal summaries. For example, "Now that we have discussed topic A, let's move on and talk about topic B."

Now that you've created the body of your presentation, it is time to move on to writing the introduction and the conclusion.

The Introduction

The introduction to your presentation serves three purposes: it grabs your audience's attention, establishes your credibility as a speaker, and previews your main points. Rather than simply announcing your topic, try to capture your audience's attention with a rhetorical question, startling statistic, or statement or anecdote. For example, the speaker might start with a question: "Can you imagine going home from work or school on the weekend and not

© Pixelbliss/Shutterstock.com

knowing if you will be getting much, if anything, to eat until the following Monday?" We caution against beginning with a joke or an attempt at humor because your opening could instead be perceived as offensive.

Next, you want to establish credibility with your audience. What knowledge or experience do you have on the subject? For our food bank speech, the speaker might establish credibility by stating: "For the past four years I have served as a board member for the food bank and have volunteered on a regular basis for many of their programs." By establishing credibility, you are letting your audience know of your interest in or connection with the topic.

The third part of the introduction is the preview. You may recall the adage: "Tell them what you are going to tell them; tell them; and tell them what you told them." Well, that still holds true. You need to tell them what you are going to tell them by way of a preview. For example, "Today I am going to enlighten you about an innovative food program that provides low-income grade-school children who rely on free lunches at school with a backpack full of nutritious, non-perishable food to be enjoyed over the weekend."

Putting it all together, your introduction would then look like the following:

Attention-getter: Can you imagine going home from work or school on Friday and not knowing if you will be getting much, if anything, to eat until the following Monday? *Establish credibility:* For the past four years I have served as a board member for the food bank and have volunteered recently for a backpack program that serves low-income students. *Preview:* Today I am going to enlighten you about an innovative food program that provides low-income, grade-school children who rely on free lunches at school, with a backpack full of nutritious, non-perishable food to be enjoyed over the weekend.

After the preview, you want to provide a signal to your audience that you are shifting to the body of your presentation. This transition smoothly moves from telling them what you are going to tell them, to telling them.

The Conclusion

Just as you should provide a transition from the introduction to the body of the speech, so should you provide a signal that moves the listener from the body to the conclusion. The conclusion is essentially the opposite of the introduction. After you have signaled to your audience that you are about to conclude ("Let's review what we have learned today…") you provide your audience with a brief review of key points. This review should remind your audience of your thesis and the purpose of the presentation.

Finally, you should plan a strong exit line that finishes the speech with impact. While many speakers end their speech with "thank you," most speech experts would caution against that. Your exit should be strong enough to stand alone. Your authors recommend a pause before your exit line, followed by your final point. Let your rate slow down and make it very clear that you are ending. You can thank the audience after they applaud! (A model

© Rawpixel/Shutterstock.com

of the outline will be provided at the end of the chapter, as well as a working page for student use.)

While delivering your presentation in an organized and coherent manner is important, you must also pay close attention to ensure your content is truthful and accurate. In the next section we will discuss ethical considerations for the speechwriter.

ETHICAL CONSIDERATIONS

As a speaker or speech writer, you want to provide factual information that comes from reliable and credible sources. This starts with the research process. Thanks to the Internet, contemporary speechwriters have information readily available at the stroke a key. "If you are going to use

© Gladskikh Tatiana/Shutterstock.com

the Internet for your research, make sure you have accurate information about the author of an article on the web, plus that person's qualifications. Often, the source is not identified, so you don't know whether the person quoted is an acknowledged expert or an eight-year-old playing on the Internet.

Be accurate and give proper credit to your sources. Improperly citing sources of information can lead to suspicion of plagiarism. Plagiarism is the unethical act of stealing or attempting to pass off another's work as your own. It denies the exclusive rights of the owner, and materially impairs these rights and the value of the work. If you are a student, plagiarism can have serious consequences. Some can be as minimal as failing an assignment, while more serious offenses can lead to dismissal from a university."* If a public relations professional is caught plagiarizing, the credibility of the person is not the only thing damaged. The entire organization can lose its reputation and face legal action.

Intellectual honesty is also an important ethical consideration. We all know in theory that lying is wrong. Yet we also know that there is a lot of false information floating around. Respect your audience by being truthful. As Mark Twain once said, "If you tell the truth, you don't have to remember anything."

Now that we have looked at ways to deal with public speaking apprehension, reviewed the key aspects of speech organization, and discussed important ethical considerations, we can move on and learn more about designing and coordinating effective visual aids for public relations presentations.

Coach's Corner: Be Positive.

Karen Kalish, president of Kalish Communications, Washington, D.C., says: "You will broadcast your feelings, whether you want to or not. If you like your audience, they will like you. Enjoy yourself and they'll enjoy themselves. If you hate it, they'll hate it. If you are uncomfortable, the audience will be, too. If you're bored, they'll go to sleep. Try to convince yourself there is nowhere else in the world you would rather be. If you don't enjoy it and get turned on by your subject, your audience won't either. If you have to, fake it till you make it."

© eurobanks/Shutterstock.com

REVIEW TERMS AND CONCEPTS

- ✓ Speech anxiety
- ✓ Energizer effect
- ✓ Positive thinking
- ✓ Specific purpose
- ✓ Thesis

- ✓ Outlining
- ✓ Transitions
- ✓ Credibility
- ✓ Plagiarism

SAMPLE SPEECH OUTLINE

Special Olympics Project Unify

Specific Purpose: To motivate my audience to support and spread awareness of Project Unify.

Thesis Statement: Project Unify is an awesome opportunity to volunteer and spread awareness about bringing people, with and without intellectual disabilities, together through sports.

Introduction

I. *Attention-getting material:* Think back to when you played sports as a kid. Were there kids on your team that had Downs Syndrome or autism? Probably not.

II. *Establish Credibility:* As many of you know I have a great passion for people with intellectual disabilities. This year I have really discovered a place in my heart for these unique and extraordinary people. What helped me find this within myself was a breakfast I went to for Special Olympics, through my internship at Hoopfest. After listening to different speakers and watching videos, I was inspired, and I knew I wanted to find out more about Special Olympics. One thing led to another and I found out about this fantastic program called Project Unify that is run through Special Olympics.

III. *Preview/thematic statement:* Even if you don't have any personal experiences with people with intellectual disabilities, I am going to tell you how you can still make a difference. Project Unify is an awesome opportunity to volunteer and spread awareness about bringing people, with and without intellectual disabilities, together through sports. The three components of Project Unify are Unified Sports where you can volunteer, Youth Activation where you can spread awareness, and Whole School Activities where you can get involved within the community and the schools.

> [transition: Let's start out by discussing Unified Sports and how you can volunteer]

Body

I. Special Olympics Unified Sports is an inclusive sports program that pairs a Special Olympics athlete (individuals with intellectual disabilities) and a partner (individuals without intellectual disabilities) to play on the same team and train together as well.
   A. Unified Sports brings equal opportunity to all athletes, which is changing the culture in school communities.
   B. The main reason Unified Sports was created was to start a program where the people with intellectual disabilities wouldn't just be sitting in the stands or on the

bench, but actually participating and playing alongside those who do not have disabilities.

C. One way you can volunteer is by being a partner with a Special Olympics athlete.

D. This partnership creates a mutually rewarding relationship and means the absolute world to them to be on the same team as you.

E. Project Unify says... "Team sports are about having fun, promoting physical health and bringing people together. Special Olympics Unified Sports teams do all of that - and shatter stereotypes about intellectual disabilities in the process."

[transition: We'll move now to another component of Project Unify, Youth Activation Committees, where you can help spread awareness]

II. Youth leaders with and without intellectual disabilities can raise awareness about inclusion by forming Project Unify clubs, also known as Youth Activation Committees within their schools.

A. This is the educational aspect to the program where volunteers go into schools to educate children about people with intellectual disabilities.

B. Clubs are started at all levels, from elementary school to the college level.

C. Learning about people with intellectual disabilities will change your whole perspective on humanity.

D. Who knows, maybe one day you might be blessed with a child with an intellectual disability and you will want them to feel just as included and accepted as everyone else.

[transition: Now what else can you actually do to help?]

III. The third component of Project Unify is Whole School Activities that are available for students to bring everyone together, support each other, and make schools more inclusive.

A. Students will lead these activities and initiatives in their school and communities, but volunteers help them.

B. Here are a few events that volunteers can help out with or support.

C. Fans in the Stands is where students with a Unified Sports team at their school can support the team by decorating their lockers, hanging posters promoting their games, and showing up with lots of school spirit.

D. The Polar Plunge "Cool School" Competition is where anyone can sign up a team to take the plunge into cold water to raise money to support athletes across the state.

E. Just to put it in perspective, each athlete pays about $600 to participate in a sports season and Special Olympics tries to have the family pay absolutely none of it.

F. So join in and be a part of the movement.

[transition: Now let's review....]

Conclusion

I. *Summary Statement:* Special Olympics Project Unify is teaching kids to be an agent of change by bringing awareness and giving people with intellectual disabilities equal opportunity through sports. Project Unify is just one step in the right direction toward making a difference.

II. *Concluding Remarks:* So let's begin to unify our community and the greater world by accepting everyone with differing abilities. Our actions create a ripple effect, whether we see it or not. What kind of ripple are you making?

Bibliography

"Project Unify." *Special Olympics Unified Sports Washington.* 28 October 2014. http://equestrianwww.specialolympicswashington.org/unified/project-unify.

APPLICATION IN ACTION

1. As a public relations professional, there will be occasions when you are giving a presentation to a group and find that your host is unprepared to formally introduce you to the group. As a result, your introduction is left to you. It is important that your audience be informed of your background, as this helps to establish your credibility as a speaker.

© Oilyy/Shutterstock.com

2. Create and deliver a speech of self-introduction.

    I. Purpose
        A. The purpose of a speech of self-introduction is to introduce yourself to your audience as you would if it were part of a longer speech.

   II. Objectives
        A. Prepare a speech of self-introduction in outline format following the format of the template and guidelines of the rubric located at the end of this chapter.
        B. Deliver a one-to-two minute speech of self-introduction from a typed outline during the next class.
        C. Practice a type of speech you will undoubtedly use later in your public relations career (practical application).
        D. Observe speeches of self-introduction during the next class.
        E. Have fun!

  III. Instructions
        A. Develop your speech around the answer to the question: What is the one thing that best describes you as a unique person?
           1. To help you answer the question above, consider these: Was there a particular person that was a great inspiration to you? Are you characterized by an activity that brings meaning to your life?
           2. Create an outline based on the information you will present. **<u>Bring a typed copy of your outline as well as the rubric to class</u>** with your name on it to give to the instructor just prior to presenting your speech.

IV. Information to be included in speech
    A. Name
    B. Major
    C. Hobbies
    D. Interests

 V. Content
    A. Positive
    B. Respectful

VI. Outline Structure and Format
    A. Three-level structure
    B. Include an Introduction, Body, and Conclusion.
    C. Follow the format contained in the rubric located at the end of this chapter.
    D. Typed

VII. Presentation
    A. **Provide a typed copy of your outline to the instructor just prior to giving your speech.**
    B. **Maximum 2 minutes in length**
    C. Vocal elements (rate, projection, inflection) and nonverbal elements (eye contact, posture, gestures, and movement) of delivery are not graded for this assignment.
    D. Don't forget to rehearse!

SPEECH OUTLINE TEMPLATE

Instructions. You will use this template to create the draft of your speech outline.
1. **Remove these two pages from your textbook.**
2. **Complete each section using a pencil (this will allow you to easily make changes).**
3. **Exchange your completed draft with your speech coach for feedback.**
4. **Submit your edited draft to your instructor on the assigned date.**

Specific Purpose:

_____

_____

Thesis Statement:

_____

_____

_____

Introduction

    I.   *Attention-getting material:*

    II.   *Establish credibility:*

    III.   *Preview/thematic statement:*

    [Transition: _____.]

Body

    I.   _____
        A.
        B.
        C.

    [Transition: _____.]

(Body continued)

II. _____

       A.

       B.

       C.

       [Transition: _____ .]

III. _____

       A.

       B.

       C.

       [Transition: _____ .]

IV. _____

       A.

       B.

       C.

       [Transition: _____ .]

Conclusion

I.   *Summary Statement:*

II.   *Concluding Remarks:*

Bibliography

1.

2.

3.

SPEECH OF SELF-INTRODUCTION EVALUATION RUBRIC

NAME _____	
CONTENT	**DELIVERY**
INTRODUCTION (5 POINTS) • Suitable opening statement, such as posing a question or using a quotation:	**EYE CONTACT** (NOT GRADED) • Directness • Randomness
BODY (10 POINTS) • Gives the audience well-developed and specific information: • Answers the question: What is the one thing that best describes you as a unique person? • Sets a positive tone for the student: • Organized: • Suitable word choice:	**VOICE** (NOT GRADED) • Natural conversational manner • Inflection/vocal variety • Rate • Projection
CONCLUSION (5 POINTS) • Ends smoothly rather than abruptly: • Suitable closing statement such as answering the question you posed in the Introduction or as simple as "Now you know _____ a little bit better:"	**BODILY ACTION** (NOT GRADED) • Posture • Gestures • Movement
OUTLINE (10 POINTS) • Typed and turned in on time (right BEFORE you present):	**VISUAL AID** (NOT GRADED) • Handling of aid • Appearance
TIME: **GRADE:**	

Credits:

Chapter 2

Visual Aids in Public Speaking

© RedKoala/Shutterstock.com

Objectives

At the completion of this chapter you should be able to:

✓ Explain the advantages and disadvantages of using a visual aid.

✓ Effectively incorporate a variety of types of visual aids.

✓ Implement tips and techniques to ensure that your visuals support your presentation.

✓ Describe and implement the SEE formula.

✓ Demonstrate your ability to use a visual aid in an informative speech.

Now that you've prepared your speech, the question arises as to whether you should use a visual aid. There are generally two schools of thought regarding the use of visual aids in public speaking. On one hand, "speech purists" believe that the speaker herself should be the sole focus of attention and they discount the use of visuals.

© lightpoet/Shutterstock.com

On the other hand, contemporary speechwriters, recognizing the current trend of an increasingly visually-oriented society, believe visual aids augment a speech in a positive way. The truth is, you can strengthen almost any kind of speech with a visual aid when the visual aid is used correctly. If you tell and *show* your audience, they'll more likely remember what you say. The specific purpose of this chapter is to provide you with tips and tactics to create effective visual aids to enhance your oral presentation.

ADVANTAGES AND DISADVANTAGES OF VISUAL AIDS

Advantages

There are three distinct advantages to using visual aids in your presentation. First, a visual aid creates interest. As the saying goes, "A picture is worth a thousand words." Second, a visual aid illustrates and reinforces the message that you are trying to get across. For example, in informative-style presentations, illustration is the major technique used to achieve audience understanding. In persuasive presentations, visual aids can increase the persuasiveness of your message by nearly 50%. Third, visual aids enhance listener retention. It has been shown that without any sort of visual reference, an audience will forget up to 70% of the content one hour after the presentation. Clearly, there are distinct advantages to using visual aids.

Disadvantages

Conversely, if a visual aid is not coordinated with what the speaker is saying or is not used properly, it will make a good speech bad and a bad speech worse. For example, in a presentation about a wildlife public relations campaign, the speaker used PowerPoint slides as a visual aid. Although the presenter was a very good public speaker, he frequently forgot to advance the PowerPoint slides to coincide with each item he spoke about, thereby causing confusion in the audience. Additionally, the presenter failed to explain the content or purpose of complex tables of information displayed on some of the slides. In the end, what promised to be a very informative presentation was ruined by poor visual aid management.

A second example involves a half-day professional workshop. The workshop presentation was heavily dependent on a series of lengthy video clips. At the beginning of the workshop, as the audience patiently waited, the presenter discovered to her horror that the video clips would not run on the equipment provided by the host organization. As a result, the presenter had to "wing it" for three hours and the audience left disappointed.

All things considered, it is our belief that visual aids should be used whenever possible. If prepared and used correctly, visual aids support what is said by the presenter and help the audience better understand what is being said. Knowing how visual aids can strengthen your presentation, let's look at some of the different kinds of visual aids.

TYPES OF VISUAL AIDS

There are a variety of visual aids available for almost any speech you want to give. These include graphs (diagrams that present numerical information), charts in which data can be represented in column, line, pie, or bar formats; maps, photographs, drawings; objects, and video clips.

We discourage the use of video clips in public relations-related speaking events for two reasons. First, you want your audience to develop a relationship with *you* and not a video clip. In most cases, at the beginning of a presentation, the audience doesn't "buy in" to the organization the speaker is representing; rather, the audience

"buys in" to the speaker herself. Video clips will inhibit this relationship-building process. Second, video clips rarely work as they are expected. The professional workshop example mentioned earlier in this chapter serves as a tragic example. Video clips generally demand a lot of computer memory, so the capability of the host computer system determines whether a video clip will run.

Objects can be very effective visual aids depending on the nature of the presentation. "If you are doing an informative-oriented presentation, such as demonstrating how to swing a golf club as part of a charity golf tournament fundraising event, you would be well advised to bring in two or three clubs along with a plastic (for safety reasons) ball and tee. In another example, if you're demonstrating easy steps in playing the guitar as part of a marketing presentation for a music store, bring along a guitar and play a tune to illustrate your basic points. If you were giving a persuasive presentation about the hazards of chewing tobacco as part of a cancer awareness campaign, you could use "Mr. Dip Lip"—a rubberized model of the human head, larynx, and chest – to graphically illustrate what happens when someone dips snuff."*

Electronic Visual Aids

PowerPoint and Prezi are popular electronic means for speakers to illustrate key ideas. Both have the advantage of brightening any talk, can display text, charts, and graphs, and can be a creative backdrop for the principal message the speaker is delivering. Many contemporary speakers use PowerPoint or Prezi slides, especially in business,

© Maxim Blinkov/Shutterstock.com

education and workshop settings. Like any visual aid, PowerPoint and Prezi can be used well or overdone. Never let your presentation be entirely dependent on electronic technology, because if it can malfunction, Murphy's Law says that it will. The audience should focus on you, the speaker, while the PowerPoint or Prezi slides should add visual interest. Remember, the substance of your speech is more important than a fancy package that calls attention to itself.

The advantages of PowerPoint include its common use and it has served as the industry standard in private and public sectors for many years. It can be stored on a flash drive, and accommodates color and photographs. Prezi, a cloud-based presentation platform, has gained popularity in recent years. It is viewed by some as eye-catching and fun. Some disadvantages to both include the need for onsite projection capability and that you often

© Matej Kastelic/Shutterstock.com

need to dim the room lights so that the slides can be easily seen.

However, good PowerPoint or Prezi slides can add overall interest. In essence, the visual effects may become more memorable than the content of the message itself. In the development of any visual aid, it's important for the speaker to keep in mind that her purpose is to inform or persuade, not entertain.

Whiteboards

Even in this electronic age, maps or posters are other items you can use to illustrate your subject. If you are going to give a talk on the advantages of yoga as a means of relaxation, you might bring in posters of calm people involved in various yoga poses. If you were speaking about the rise and fall of the stock market, graphs and charts would help your audience grasp your key ideas.

Even self-drawn aids on a whiteboard can help make the material stick and also work as a means of displaying comments and input in an interactive or brainstorming type of presentation.

Whiteboards are appealing as a low-tech backup if a PowerPoint or Prezi fails to display. Also, the use of whiteboards lends to an overall multimedia approach. When used in conjunction with an electronic method, such as PowerPoint, it provides some variety for the audience. One word of caution when using the

© lightpoet/Shutterstock.com

whiteboard is that you have to turn your back to the audience when writing. Also, when pointing to something on the whiteboard, or any other visual aid for that matter, the presenter must use care to point with the hand closest to the board. Using the hand opposite the board will cause the speaker to cross her arm across her body, causing a barrier between the speaker and the audience.

Now that we've looked at some different types of visual aids, let's talk about their preparation and delivery.

PREPARATION AND DELIVERY TIPS

If you're going to create a visual of any kind, here are some tips to make sure it supports, rather than inhibits, your presentation.

Viewability

Simplicity and viewability are the watchwords for visual-aid slide development. With regard to simplicity, eliminate slide clutter by displaying only essential information. Provide bulleted key concepts rather than word-for-word paragraphs. Minimize the use of audible and visual animations of text in slides because animations are often more distracting than entertaining. Also, because they draw computer memory, they may slow down the slides.

> **Perception is Reality**
>
> In spite of all of your work in preparing a visual aid, if it cannot be easily read and understood by your audience, it will be viewed by that audience as a lack of preparation and consideration on your part and will diminish your credibility as a presenter.

Viewability is important. If your audience can't see what you've created, your visual aids serve no purpose. Viewability involves effective contrast between text and background. Font style and size are additional considerations, as the slide should be able to be easily read by the person farthest from the screen. Finally, balance is important; this means don't overload a slide with too much content.

Color increases listener content recognition by over 70%; therefore, a PowerPoint or Prezi slide should include color. The color scheme should consist of light-colored print and a dark background or vice versa in order to provide sufficient contrast so the audience can easily read the content. A note of caution: Just because the slide colors and contrast look good on the computer monitor it doesn't mean it will look that same way when projected onto the larger screen. Therefore, it is absolutely essential that you view it

© Matej Kastelic/Shutterstock.com

projected onto a screen, viewing as an audience would, before finalizing your slide background and text colors.

Frequently overlooked by presenters are visual considerations for members of the audience who are colorblind. You need to assume that there will be at least one colorblind person in the audience. According to the American Optometric Association's website, people with color vision deficiency "have difficulty differentiating between particular shades of red and green (most common) or blues and yellows (less common)." For instance, avoid using red text on a black background.

Font style should be consistent throughout and consist of upper/lower-case text (all capital letters give an angry appearance). Use the following font size protocol when creating your slide: Title slide as 36 point; subtitles as 24 point; and, other text as 18 point. Bullet points should be used sparingly to summarize key points and used in concert with images, such as photographs. Images improve listener recognition and recall and, given the growing visual emphasis of today's society, should be used in place of the written word whenever describing or comparing and contrasting something. If you are displaying text documents, such as policies, pages from the employee handbook, etc., be sure to set the monitor's zoom level to at least 120%.

Simplicity in content is also important. The primary purpose of the visual aid is to illustrate in more graphic detail what you're saying in the presentation. For example, if you're talking about the advantage of volunteering with the nonprofit organization that you represent, and you display text-heavy, difficult-to-read slides about the volunteer activities, you could defeat your purpose.

© Peter Bernik/Shutterstock.com

Familiarity

"Few things are more frustrating for a speaker than a visual aid that fails to work. Let's say you've prepared a PowerPoint explaining the advantages of driving an economy car as part of an environmental awareness campaign that you are leading. You have created the PowerPoint, but never tested it on the host system before delivering the presentation."* You'll have far more peace of mind by testing the host audiovisual equipment ahead of time. Do this by running the visual aid on the host's system *before* the presentation to make sure the computer software is compatible and that the projector works properly. Remember Murphy's Law and anticipate in advance that the computer or projector won't work and have a contingency plan, such as a portable system that you bring or a paper copy of all the slides, in case that happens.

Delivery

When actually delivering your presentation with visuals, use the SEE formula: Show, Explain, and Eye contact.

<u>Show</u> the visual aid only when you're making a specific point about it. If you give a presentation about the corporate social responsibility initiatives your company is involved in, make sure the slide matches the point you're talking about at the time. For example, if you finish talking about your company's adopt-a-highway litter-removal program and have the slide of a chart showing the reduction of office paper usage over the past five years, you'll confuse your audience. We recommend inserting the words "change slide" in your speaker notes in the appropriate places to serve as a cue for you to move to the next slide. A great tactic to use to keep your audience focused on you instead of on the screen when you are talking between slides is to place blank slides between content slides. This shifts the audience's focus back to you the speaker. Additionally, if you want the title of your presentation to be a surprise, place a blank

slide immediately preceding the title slide for your audience to see before you actually begin the presentation.

<u>Explain</u> your visual to the audience if it is in the form of a chart, graph, etc., that contains information not readily apparent or easily understood. The wildlife public relations campaign example mentioned earlier in this

© Rawpixel/Shutterstock.com

35

chapter showed the necessity of explaining complex visuals to the audience. Don't presume everyone understands.

Eye contact must be maintained with your audience. Talk to your audience, not to your visual. Use your slides as a point of reference and not as a script. "It's easy to talk directly to the visual aid while you're showing it, rather than talking to your audience."* If a speaker turns her back to the audience when displaying a slide, it's harder to hear the speaker and the speaker will lose eye contact—the connection—with the audience. When referring to the slides, if a speaker cannot directly face the audience, then she should at least stand sideways, so she can make reference to the visual aid while maintaining her visual connection with the audience.

© Rawpixel/Shutterstock.com

In this chapter we examined the role of visual aids in an oral presentation. We explored the advantages and disadvantages of using a visual aid in an oral presentation and examined various visual aids. We then identified steps in preparation and delivery. In the next chapter we will explore the different kinds of speeches public relations professionals deliver, as well as some specific techniques for increasing your presentation's effectiveness.

We've all heard the old saying that "the show must go on." The level of expectation in today's visually-oriented audiences is that a visual aid will be presented electronically through applications such as PowerPoint or Prezi. Both are computer system- and projector-dependent in order to be displayed. You must have a backup plan if the host computer system will not run your presentation (recall the workshop example earlier in the chapter) or if power is lost to the system, there is a lock-up, or the very common problem of the projector bulb burning out. If possible bring a portable system as a backup, but at the very least, have a printout of your slides. It is always preferable to have audiovisual technicians standing by if at all possible. Remember: If technology can fail, it almost always will, so prepare for problems. Hope for the best and plan for the worst.

© eurobanks/Shutterstock.com

REVIEW TERMS AND CONCEPTS

✓ Visual aid advantages

✓ Visual aid disadvantages

✓ Objects

✓ Electronic visual aids

✓ Whiteboard

✓ Viewability

✓ Familiarity

✓ SEE formula

APPLICATION IN ACTION

1. Given the highly visual orientation of today's audiences, effective public relations presentations always include a visual aid. A visual aid increases audience interest and message retention.

2. Illustration is the major technique in informative speaking. Create and deliver an informative speech about a successful

© Oilyy/Shutterstock.com

marketing, media or public relations campaign incorporating an electronic visual aid.

   I.   Purpose
       A. The purpose of an informative speech is to provide interesting, useful, and unique information to your audience.

  II.   Objectives
       A. Prepare an informative speech in 2- to 4-page outline following the format of the template and guidelines of the rubric located at the end of this chapter.
       B. Deliver a 5- to 7-minute informative speech from an outline using an electronic visual aid.
       C. Observe informative speeches given by other members of the class.
       D. Practice researching, writing, organizing and speaking skills.
       E. Practice a type of speech you will use later in your professional career (practical application).

  III.   Instructions
       A. Topic selection must be a marketing, media or public relations campaign that has occurred within the last 10 years.
       B. Library/Internet research is required for this speech. <u>You must have at least 3 sources listed in your bibliography at the end of your outline.</u>
       C. Create an outline based on the information you will present. **<u>Bring a typed paper copy of your outline as well as the rubric to class</u>** with your name on it to give to the instructor just prior to presenting your speech.

SPEECH OUTLINE TEMPLATE

Instructions. You will use this template to create the draft of your speech outline.
1. **Remove these two pages from your textbook.**
2. **Complete each section using a pencil (this will allow you to easily make changes).**
3. **Exchange your completed draft with your speech coach for feedback.**
4. **Submit your edited draft to your instructor on the assigned date.**

Specific Purpose:

_____

_____

Thesis Statement:

_____

_____

_____

Introduction

    I.   *Attention-getting material:*

    II.   *Establish credibility:*

    III.   *Preview/thematic statement:*

       [Transition: _____.]

Body

    I.   _____
         A.
         B.
         C.

       [Transition: _____.]

(Body continued)

II. _____
    A.
    B.
    C.

    [Transition: _____ .]

III. _____
    A.
    B.
    C.

    [Transition: _____ .]

IV. _____
    A.
    B.
    C.

    [Transition: _____ .]

Conclusion

I.   *Summary Statement:*

II.   *Concluding Remarks:*

Bibliography

1.
2.
3.

INFORMATIVE SPEECH EVALUATION RUBRIC

CONTENT	DELIVERY
NAME _____	

CONTENT	DELIVERY
INTRODUCTION (10 POINTS) • Opening statement that <u>doesn't announce topic</u> (Attention getter) • Establishes credibility • Previews the speech • Thesis Statement	**EYE CONTACT** (10 POINTS) • Directness • Randomness
BODY (10 POINTS) • 2- to 4-page typewritten outline following the three-level, full-sentence format (no paragraphs), numbering, and general appearance in the textbook • Contains 2 to 5 main points in a clear organizational pattern (time order, topic order, or logical reasons) • Major points of the speech are linked with <u>transitions</u>	**VOICE & MOVEMENT** (5 POINTS) • Projection • Minimal Vocalized Pauses • Posture • Gestures
CONCLUSION (5 POINTS) • Summarizes the main points of the speech • Ends with a quotation, story, or ties back to opening sentence ("clincher")	**TIME** (10 POINTS) • Conformed to 5- to 7-minute time limit
VISUAL AID (10 POINTS) • Handling of Aid • Appearance • Contains at least 5 slides	
TIME: **GRADE:**	

Coaching for Informative Speech

Assignment: Remove this page from your text and bring to class on the day that your speaking partner presents his or her speech. During the presentation, take notes based on the questions provided below. Then, write a one- to two-page critique discussing your answers to those questions as you assess your speaking partner. This should be written in paragraph form.

1. How well did the speaker describe the successful campaign?

2. How effective was the speaker's use of visuals? Explain.

3. How effectively did the speaker grab your attention? How well did the conclusion summarize the presentation?

4. Was the speech organized in accordance with the outline template and were transitions used effectively?

5. "Comment on the speaker's voice, gestures, and facial expressions? Were they used appropriately to engage the audience? Was the voice modulated in pitch and volume?"**

Credits:

Chapter 3

Presentations and Techniques Commonly Used in Public Relations

Objectives

At the completion of this chapter you should be able to:

✓ Describe the specific types of presentations that public relations professionals typically make.

✓ Explain the benefits of storytelling as a technique.

✓ Understand the different techniques of persuasion and their use.

✓ Demonstrate your ability to deliver a speech of goodwill.

All along this text has been emphasizing the importance of preparing the speech writer or corporate spokesperson to deliver effective presentations. This chapter will focus on the types of presentations that public relations

© photographer/Shutterstock.com

professionals typically make, and provide some recommended techniques that are proven to make the speaker even more effective.

TYPES OF PRESENTATIONS

Presentations and speech writing are important public relations tools that help the organization reach its key audiences. Whether the organization is announcing a new product or responding to a product recall, the goal is to maintain, and even enhance, the organization's positive reputation. So what kinds of speeches do public relations professionals make? Let's start with the "feel good" speeches.

Goodwill

A speech of goodwill is intended to create goodwill, or a favorable view toward an organization or corporation. Toastmasters describes this type of speech as one in which "goodwill toward an organization, club, company, or other group is created by giving the audience information about it and its role in your community." The goal is not necessarily to get your audience to join or support anything, but to have greater awareness and a positive outlook toward the organization. The audience can be internal publics including staff or organizational leaders.

A goodwill presentation can take many forms. For example, the presentation may be part of a tradition or ceremony where an employee or group of employees are honored for the work they do in the community. A goodwill presentation could also take the form of an after-dinner

© photographer/Shutterstock.com

presentation that takes a light-hearted approach, such as a roast. When all is said and done, the speech is intended to make people feel good about themselves and the organization with which they are associated.

Image Building

An image-building presentation might be designed to promote goodwill, but it can also have a persuasive intent. According to BusinessTown.com "an image-building presentation represents an effort to position a company, an organization, or an individual as a leader in an industry or field, as an expert on a certain subject, as a good guy, or as a good neighbor." Usually the presentation is linked to some

© photographer/Shutterstock.com

sort of sales effort, so the platform is used for public relations publicity purposes and it is likely that the media will be invited. For instance, the CEO of a long-standing and well-known high tech company recently announced the rollout of an exciting and innovative product using a well-designed presentation and professionally crafted slides in front of a live audience, including the media. His presentation was simplified for audience consumption and understanding. The very positive response of the audience, seen in their resounding applause, reflected their excitement about the new product. Additionally, this response demonstrated an understanding and appreciation of the presentation, which served to create, or reinforce a very positive image of the company.

Crisis Communication

According to Kathleen Fearn-Banks (*Crisis Communications: A Casebook Approach*), "A crisis is a major occurrence with a potentially negative outcome affecting the organization, company, or industry, as well as its publics, products, services, or good name." It seems as though there is a new public relations crisis in the news almost every day.

While we could write an entire book on examples of how public relations professionals have badly handled crisis responses, we want you and your organization to avoid becoming the next classic case study of what not to do. Let's focus on what you should do.

© photographer/Shutterstock.com

In the event that a potentially damaging situation has occurred, your goal as the public relations specialist is to lessen the damage that is already done, or prevent an incident from ballooning into a full-blown crisis. Hopefully, your organization already has a crisis communication plan in place. When a crisis has occurred, the speaker or speech writer must get to work quickly to prepare a response. You must determine your purpose. What do you hope to accomplish with the presentation? Do you need to inform the audience as to what has happened or do they already know? It's pretty difficult to keep much of anything a secret nowadays, given the speed of social media. So, maybe your purpose is to calm your audience's fears or to give information about how an incident is playing out. It is equally important for you to know what you can't say. Perhaps there are legal or business proprietary reasons why you are not at liberty to tell all.

One of the most important things the speaker needs to do is to show care, compassion, and concern, whether it is for an individual, his or her family, or for the general public. Next, the spokesperson needs to truthfully provide all relevant information. This goes back to our journalism training. You need to get the who,

© photographer/Shutterstock.com

what, why, when, and where out in the open right away. If your organization made a mistake, admit it. Also, you would be well-served to admit that you may not have all the information the public wants at that particular time, but that you will provide further information as it becomes available. And, by all means, be sincere. Audiences want to know that you actually care about them. Finally, assure your audience that your organization will make the situation right. According to Sandra Fathi (*PR Insider: The Executive Apology, Avoid Making it Worse Once You've Already Screwed Up*), "An immediate, sincere apology that commits to taking action will resonate with key audiences and influencers and can be effective in mitigating damage and salvaging a reputation." Quick and accurate information reduces uncertainty, and in many cases, your response can actually create greater trust and/or brand loyalty. This advice goes for communicating with both internal and external publics.

Apology

There are times when individuals or organizations must "right a wrong." This might begin with an apology to their publics. As we pointed out, you must be sincere. Sometimes public apologies miss the mark. They blame the victim, saying something like, "I'm sorry if I offended anyone," or they make it about themselves, "I will regret this for the rest of my life." Others wait too long to apologize and a situation that could have quickly been diffused escalates to the point of damaging an individual's or corporation's reputation.

© photographer/Shutterstock.com

The intent and tone of the apology are crucial components. If the apology sounds like a legal brief, you have missed the mark. As with a response to a crisis, the speech of apology needs to be sincere in your word choice and in your nonverbal delivery. Eye contact is essential. If you read directly from a script and avoid looking at your audience, you might as well just tell your audience that they shouldn't believe you.

Also, use social media to back your apology. Put it out there that you are taking positive steps as you move forward from the unfortunate situation. Increase audience awareness of the steps you are taking. As Diedre Breakenridge, CEO of Pure Performance Communications says, "A meaningful apology, backed by supportive measures, will keep your reputation and relationships intact."

We've discussed the typical kinds of presentations PR professionals either write for others or deliver themselves. We recognize that public relations spokespersons may be called upon to represent their organizations in press conferences, and we will discuss this in great detail in Chapter 7, Speaking to the Media. The next section will cover two proven techniques that

serve to enhance the overall effectiveness of your presentations: storytelling and persuasion.

TECHNIQUES

Storytelling

The presentation that drones on and on

with facts alone can be, to put it bluntly, boring.

But stories can bring the presentation to life. Who

doesn't like a good story? We've been asking

people to tell us stories since we were children.

© photographer/Shutterstock.com

Stories can conjure up curiosity or they can help a complicated concept make better sense.

Stories ignite feelings. When your audience has an emotional reaction to what you are telling

them, they are more likely to remember what you talked about. Whether the story makes you

laugh or feel empathetic toward someone or a situation, that story has engaged your senses. The

more senses we can engage, the longer the message will be remembered. Some of the best

speakers are the best storytellers. Former President Ronald Reagan was known as "the Great

Communicator" because he always wove stories into his messages. What you may not know is

that he was an actor before he became president, so he had some good practice with storytelling.

If you want to be quoted, tell a story.

Stories help shape brands. People are interested in reading stories about other people. For

example, a pharmaceutical organization that announces a ground-breaking vaccine could

"humanize and personalize" this discovery by writing a profile story about the research team

members that created the vaccine and their experiences in the vaccine development process. By telling stories, you are likely to sell more of your product and persuade more effectively. We will talk more about techniques of persuasion later on in this chapter.

Personal stories are best. You know the story because it is *your* story. Personal stories that create vivid images in your audience's minds or take them on a journey make the presentation memorable. You want your listener to feel as if she was there with you.

© photographer/Shutterstock.com

Utilizing such techniques as tossing in an unexpected twist, or pausing to ask, "and can you imagine what happened next?" can keep your listener engaged. On the other hand, some stories are simply too painful to tell and should be avoided, as the speaker could be overtaken with emotion and not be able to recover enough to finish the presentation smoothly.

Not all stories that speakers tell will be about themselves. They can be about others as well. Perhaps you might want to create empathy and you tell a story about something that happened to someone you know. Stories told about others can help your audience to empathize or experience someone else's experiences and emotions.

"Of course, you want to make sure your story relates to your key messages. Find stories that reinforce the points you want to make."*** If possible, keep a file of stories that you can draw from for future presentations. There's nothing wrong with reviving an old story with a new audience and a new presentation. Just don't make the mistake of telling the same story twice to the same audience.

Not all people can tell stories well, so you definitely want to rehearse. You may need to edit your story due to time constraints. Just make sure the story is still worth telling after editing it. As the storyteller, you do have some creative license, but just be careful not to embellish to the point of not being believable. Furthermore, you do not have to be funny to tell a story, but if you are and the context is appropriate, humor can boost audience receptivity. But forced humor can be both disastrous and embarrassing for both the speaker and the audience. If you question your material, try it out on someone who can give you an honest opinion. This is what we call reputation damage control.

© photographer/Shutterstock.com

"Finally, avoid 'winging it.'"*** By this we mean don't make it up as you go along. We've all heard the speaker who tells an "unintended story that ends up stealing his thunder for a point he intended to make later in the speech."*** Winging it can end up taking up too much speaker time or it can lead to the speaker straying so far off track that he will have difficulty returning to his key point. Our advice: don't wing it. Stick with what you have planned and you won't ever need to worry about straying from your point.

In sum, stories can add life to a presentation and enhance audience retention. In this next section we will explore persuasion as another technique to use in your public relations presentations.

Persuasion

There has been a long-standing debate over whether public relations professionals are "spin doctors" without regard for the truth and whether or not they utilize persuasion or "propaganda" in their messages. As in any profession, there are bad apples, however, the vast majority of public relations professionals abide by the profession's ethical standards. In this section, we advocate that *ethical* persuasion is an important key to successful public relations.

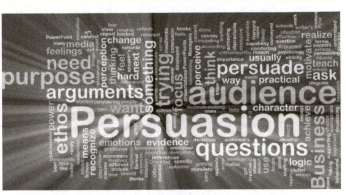

© photographer/Shutterstock.com

Persuasion is at the heart of most public relations messages. You may be attempting to convince your board of directors to support a change in a company policy or trying to motivate voters to support your candidate for office. Persuasive messages may be directed at both internal and external audiences. The content of persuasive messages range from simple to complex, the latter as might be seen in a political campaign.

Persuasion is about seeking audience agreement with your point of view or the point of view that you represent. Public relations professionals utilize persuasion in dealing with the media, politics, and with internal and external publics. Let's look at some particularly effective techniques of persuasion.

Seeking agreement by leading your audience through a series of statements with which they can agree helps win your audience to your way of thinking. The speaker might lead the listeners through the following: "We all agree that conserving electricity is good for the economy and the environment. We all agree that conserving energy in our homes means lower energy bills. We all agree that by using programmable thermostats we can conserve energy by turning down the temperature while we are away or asleep and in turn, lower our heating bills. Who doesn't want to save money while protecting the environment?" Notice the logical progression of points of agreement.

Structured choices are, according to Wilcox and Reber (2013), "a technique that "force[s] the audience to choose between A and B." A political candidate may ask, "Do you want this country to continue increasing the national debt or do you want lower taxes and more money in your pocket?" In this case the speaker persuades by seeking agreement through a series of choices.

© photographer/Shutterstock.com

Wilcox and Reber (2013) also suggest that the speaker "ask for more, settle for less." This approach is commonly used during union negotiations with management. The union official will ask for a larger than expected raise for union employees and then settle at a dollar value that they realistically hoped to obtain.

A persuasive presentation can be either one-sided or offer several sides of an issue. There are pros and cons to both approaches. In general, when you know your audience is already in agreement with your position, the one-sided approach works well. Often you will face the dilemma of whether to present just your side of the argument and run the risk of having a weak position, or bring up opposing arguments, which takes time away from developing your argument during your presentation. We recommend presenting both sides of the argument when the audience is hostile, well-educated, or will be exposed to counterarguments.

> **Perception is Reality**
> People act on their own perception of facts. Therefore, as the public relations spokesperson, you must strive to shape audiences' perceptions based on facts, rather than opinions.

We are all consumers. We are consumers of products and we are consumers of information. We buy things based on logic, emotion, or both. A good salesperson sizes up the consumer to figure out if he or she is going to be more easily swayed by information such as facts, statistics, survey results, etc., or by how the product or service will make him or her feel, such as secure, healthy, good looking, etc. It all goes back to audience analysis. Know who you are talking to and what approach will work best. If you don't know your audience's stance, you will want to have a blend of logical and emotional appeals so you have a better chance of gaining agreement from a majority of your audience.

Including examples and testimonials in your presentation is also a powerful persuasive technique. For example, say that you are head of development for a nonprofit organization that is raising money for expanding their mental health counseling services. Testimonials from clients who have benefitted from those services can have a strong influence on prospective donors in the audience.

In this chapter we have looked at several different kinds of presentations that public relations professionals will write for others or deliver themselves. We also discussed storytelling and persuasion as two useful techniques that greatly enhance the effectiveness of public relations presentations. In the next chapter we will examine the notion of perception as it relates to the speaker and the audience.

As a speech coach, encourage your speakers to keep a file of stories and anecdotes for a variety of topics on hand so they can be used for future presentations. Sometimes the speaker can revive an "old" story if the audience and/or location is new and different. With a collection of personal stories, the speaker will be more apt to connect with the audience and leave a longer-lasting impression.

© eurobanks/Shutterstock.com

REVIEW TERMS AND CONCEPTS

✓ Goodwill presentation

✓ Image-building presentation

✓ Crisis communication presentation

✓ Speech of apology

✓ Storytelling

✓ Persuasion

✓ Seeking agreement

✓ Structured choices

APPLICATION IN ACTION

1. Whether the organization is announcing a new product or responding to a product recall, the goal is to maintain, and even enhance, the organization's positive reputation.

© Oilyy/Shutterstock.com

2. A speech of goodwill is a public relations strategy intended to create goodwill, or a favorable view toward an organization or corporation. Create and deliver a speech of goodwill about the benefits of an organization or company of your choice.

   I.   Purpose
        A. The primary purpose of a speech of goodwill is to generate positive feelings toward you and your product, service, or organization.

  II.   Objectives
        A. Prepare a speech of goodwill in a 2- to 3-page outline following the format of the template and guidelines of the rubric located at the end of this chapter.
        B. Deliver a 4- to 5-minute speech of goodwill from an outline using an electronic visual aid.
        C. Observe speeches of goodwill given by other members of the class.
        D. Practice researching, writing, organizing and speaking skills.
        E. Practice a type of speech you may use later in your professional career (practical application).

 III.   Instructions
        A. You are the public relations spokesperson for a company of your choice.
        B. Your presentation must build your public's favorable feeling toward you in a subtle, indirect way and generate positive feelings toward you and your product, service, or organization.
        C. Give your audience factual information about the organization and its role in the community.
        D. Remember, this is not a sales pitch, but the performance of a service that is related to the business or cause (need not be an organization that you are associated with.)

E. Create an outline (bibliography included) based on the information you will present. **<u>Bring a typed paper copy of your outline as well as the rubric to class</u>** with your name on it to give to the instructor just prior to presenting your speech.

SPEECH OUTLINE TEMPLATE

Instructions. You will use this template to create the draft of your speech outline.

    1. Remove these two pages from your textbook.

    2. Complete each section using a pencil (this will allow you to easily make changes).

    3. Exchange your completed draft with your speech coach for feedback.

    4. Submit your edited draft to your instructor on the assigned date.

Specific Purpose:

_____

_____

Thesis Statement:

_____

_____

_____

Introduction

    I.   *Attention-getting material:*

    II.   *Establish credibility:*

    III.   *Preview/thematic statement:*

        [Transition: _____.]

Body

    I.   _____

        A.

        B.

        C.

        [Transition: _____.]

(Body continued)
    II. _____

        A.
        B.
        C.

        [Transition: _____.]

    III. _____

        A.
        B.
        C.

        [Transition: _____.]

    IV. _____

        A.
        B.
        C.

        [Transition: _____.]

Conclusion

    I.   *Summary Statement:*

    II.   *Concluding Remarks:*

Bibliography

1.
2.
3.

SPEECH OF GOODWILL EVALUATION RUBRIC

NAME _____	
CONTENT	**DELIVERY**
INTRODUCTION (10 POINTS) • Opening statement that <u>doesn't announce topic</u> (Attention getter) • Establishes credibility • Previews the speech • Thesis Statement	**EYE CONTACT** (10 POINTS) • Directness • Randomness
BODY (10 POINTS) • 2- to 3-page typewritten outline following the three-level, full-sentence format (no paragraphs), numbering, and general appearance in the textbook • Contains evidence of solid research • Builds goodwill towards the organization by presenting factual information • Major points of the speech are linked with <u>transitions</u>	**VOICE & MOVEMENT** (5 POINTS) • Projection • Minimal Vocalized Pauses • Posture • Gestures
CONCLUSION (5 POINTS) • Summarizes the main points of the speech • Ends with a quotation, story, or ties back to opening sentence ("clincher")	**TIME** (10 POINTS) • Conformed to 4- to 5-minute time limit
VISUAL AID (10 POINTS) • Handling of Aid • Appearance	
TIME: **GRADE:**	

Coaching for Goodwill Speech

Assignment: Remove this page from your text and bring to class on the day that your speaking partner presents his or her speech. During the presentation, take notes based on the questions provided below. Then, write a one- to two-page critique discussing your answers to those questions as you assess your speaking partner. This should be written in paragraph form.

1. "How well did the speech fit the interests of the audience? Explain."**

2. "Comment on the speaker's research. Was it thorough? Relevant? Factual?"**

3. "Assuming you had no knowledge of the speaker's subject, would you have been favorably impressed by the speech? Would you feel friendly toward the organization the speaker represented?"**

4. "How did the visual aid(s) facilitate audience understanding? How effectively was it used?"**

5. "If you were the organization's president, would you choose this speaker to represent the organization in a series of community meetings? Why? Why not?"**

6. Comment on the speaker's non-verbal delivery. Include comments on eye contact, gestures, movement, vocal variety, and overall effectiveness.

Credits:

**Toastmasters *Advanced Communication Series Public Relations*

***Cohen, S.D. *On the Path to Success*. San Diego. 2012.

Listener Perception

Chapter 4

© Rido/Shutterstock.com

Objectives

At the completion of this chapter you should be able to:

- ✓ Understand the notion of listener perception.

- ✓ Explain the key components of the perception process.

- ✓ Describe the influence of perception on effective message delivery in public speaking.

- ✓ Demonstrate in an informative speech your understanding of the three parts of the sense-making process an audience employs when listening to a presentation, i.e., selection, organization, and interpretation.

At this point, you've learned the basics of speech organization and development of visual aids. Now we will look into various aspects of our audience as receivers. The purpose of this chapter is to explore the notion of listener perception as it relates to speech writing and delivery for public relations.

BACKGROUND

You've no doubt heard the adage "perception is reality." The point is that people tend to consider what they perceive or view in a given situation as reality. This is especially relevant in crisis communication situations. A lesson frequently learned the hard way in the public relations profession is that an organizational crisis can be initiated simply by a *perception* of the media or publics that the organization did not react in an appropriate manner. The severity of the crisis lies in the eyes of the beholder. The meanings people attach, and the actions they take that are based on their perceptions have become one of the most important considerations in contemporary public relations messaging.

The brain selects information depending on individual needs and interests. "In daily life, people are constantly faced with situations in which two listeners may be hearing the exact same presentation or conversation, but walk away with two very different

© mast3r/Shutterstock.com

versions of what took place."* For example, your Human Resources Director announces a change to a less-expensive employee medical benefits provider. The corporate leadership will perceive this as a positive move because of cost savings to the company. Conversely, the employees will perceive this as a threat to their ability to choose a caregiver. Even though everyone in the company hears the same message, perceptions differ depending on individual needs and interests.

THE PERCEPTION PROCESS

© gary yim/Shutterstock.com

"Perception is an active process by which people assign meaning to their experiences. Psychologists traditionally divide experience into two classes: sensation and perception. Seeing a red octagon on a pole on a street is a sensation, but seeing that red octagon as a STOP sign is a perception. The process of perception involves the selection, organization, and interpretation of sensory data that helps people make sense of the world. Beebe (2001) claims perception is the arousal of any of our senses, and interpersonal perception is the process by which we decide what people are like, and give meaning to their actions."*

The process of perception plays a key role in building relationships with others. The Public Relations Society of America (PRSA) website describes public relations as a "communication process emphasizing mutually beneficial relationships." Building these relationships requires interaction with people, either one-on-one or in a group setting. The participants assign meaning to these interactions or experiences, whether they occur "one-on-one" or "one-on-many," as is the case in public speaking.

As a public relations speech writer, presenter, and executive coach, it is essential to remember that audience perception of the message and the messenger (whether that is you or your boss) greatly influences the successful delivery and receipt of the message. How do we accomplish this? Let's start by looking closely at the three parts of the sense-making process an audience employs when listening to the message: selection, organization, and interpretation.

Selection

Every day you are forced to choose from or identify stimuli that come your way, and then decide to which you will pay attention. "This is called selection, or selective attention—that is, you can process only a certain amount of what is going on around you at a given moment. While these selections are not necessarily conscious, people do exercise some control over what they perceive."* For example, your audience will tend to pay attention to those stimuli that are of interest to them or with which they are familiar, based on past experiences. Past experience will play a major role in what your audience perceives or chooses to perceive. For example, let's say you are the public relations director presenting on behalf of a diabetes awareness organization for the purpose of raising money for diabetes research and education. Your audience members that have diabetes, or know someone with diabetes, such as a family member, will be more apt to pay attention and motivated to contribute given their experience with the disease.

© Dikiiy/Shutterstock.com

Organization

Once stimuli have come your audience's way, they must organize them in some form that has meaning for them. Holding general ideas about people, places and things, or maintaining a generalized idea of how an event should unfold, help your audience make sense of the information. "While many factors influence the organizational phase of the perception process, the degree of ambiguity of the information in the message as well as the listener's emotional state are of particular significance in public relations messaging. As information becomes more ambiguous, the chances for perceptual errors increase. Think about the time when you needed to look at a situation two or three times, only to realize that what you thought you saw was not

71

actually there."* The fact that messages have more than one way of being organized, along with individual variation in experiences with particular stimuli, only leads to further confusion and misunderstanding by the intended audience. In their social information processing theory,

Salancik and Pfeefer (1978) point out that in ambiguous situations, individuals rely heavily on socially derived interpretations of events or issues. This can occur in a public speaking situation where individuals in the audience, when presented with ambiguous issues, discuss those issues with other members of their social network, in this case, other audience members.

"An audience's emotional state may also influence the way they organize sensory stimuli and leave themselves open to perceptual errors."* It has been

---

Perception is Reality

As a public relations practitioner, it is important to note that an audience's perception is their reality. For example, in a crisis, an organization may believe they are adequately addressing the problem; however, this makes no difference in the big scheme of things if the organization's publics and stakeholders perceive otherwise. It is incumbent on you, the public relations presenter, to determine what perception your publics hold in any given situation and address it accordingly. For example, a couple of decades ago, a high-tech manufacturer's newly-introduced computer processor chip contained a flaw that caused an error to occur during complex mathematical calculations. The manufacturer's upper-level management believed that the issue was insignificant because the majority of the general public didn't do complex mathematical calculations and either would not notice or not care. Management was wrong. The end users (like you and me) perceived the flaw as a deficiency with the product. The chip manufacturer finally agreed to recall the chip at a cost of millions of dollars. It had to deal with the ensuing public relations fiasco and spent years regaining customer trust.

---

found in certain instances that when an organization is in a crisis situation, its audience tends to react emotionally instead processing factual information. For example, when a cruise line experienced mechanical problems onboard a number of its ships, the company attempted to explain its lack of response by citing mechanical causes, yet the audiences were instead focused on the unsanitary and uncomfortable living conditions that existed aboard ship as reported by the passengers to   the media.

Interpretation

"Once an audience has selected and organized sensory data, they need to give that data meaning. Interpretation is giving meaning to that information."* As with the selection phase, past experience plays a key role in interpreting situations. For example, an audience may find it difficult to trust a speaker who has been involved in a widely-known ethical scandal in the past. The audience probably would interpret the speaker's previous behavior as something typical of that person, which, in turn, adversely affects the audience's perception of the speaker's credibility, which diminishes the speaker's likability in the eyes of the audience.

© bbevren/Shutterstock.com

As previously mentioned, an audience's emotional state can affect how they organize perceptual stimuli. "The interpretation process can also be influenced by an audience's emotional state."* For example, your audience is comprised of employees who have just been informed that their pay will be cut 10 percent because of a drop in last year's profits. You, as the public relations director, have been told by the company vice president to gather and inform the employees that the organization will be redesigning its jobs in an attempt to streamline operations to improve next year's earnings. The employees' already negative emotional state prevents them from understanding that job redesign is an effort by management to save, instead of ultimately eliminate, the employees' jobs.

Social influence and context also play an important role in an audience's interpretation of information. Audience members are easily aroused by the emotional expressions of others. An

© Stuart Jenner/Shutterstock.com

individual's attitude may be affected by another's interpretation of events or information. According to social information processing theory, social context generally affects an individual's attitudes by focusing an individual's attention on certain information which makes that information more relevant. Of importance to the public relations presenter, this so-called relevant, often emotion-based, information can interfere with factual information that an individual uses to form an explanation. A number of years ago a top-end bicycle lock manufacturer found this out the hard way when word spread through social and traditional media that one of its expensive locks could be opened with a ballpoint pen. The company didn't immediately view this situation as a crisis and didn't respond right away. To its detriment, its customers, who spent a lot of money for an apparently faulty lock, began returning the locks in droves and formed an irrevocable negative perception of the manufacturer. The company eventually responded by offering a no-cost exchange for its locks, but it was too late to change the opinion and perceptions of some of its customers.

Assumptions and Barriers

We just learned that perceptions are influenced by the three parts of the sense-making process. "In this next section, we explore additional factors that affect the accuracy of perceptions. People tend to make assumptions about people and situations and use barriers that distort perceptual interpretations."* As a public relations speech writer and presenter, simple awareness of these processes is important to understanding potential barriers to your message reaching your audience.

Halo Effect

"This perceptual error occurs when a particular characteristic or individual trait profoundly influences all other impressions of the person."* In essence, it simply means that the first impression becomes the only impression to prevail. For example, think of a presentation where the speaker was very smartly dressed and presenting on behalf of a charitable cause. Her appearance alone leaves you with

© Photo Africa/Shutterstock.com

the impression that the person must be ethical and honest as well. Later you learned that the ideas presented by the speaker were an attempt to obtain your money through a donation for purely personal purposes without any intent to use that donation in the manner described in the presentation. What you didn't notice in the presentation was the speaker's lack of specific knowledge about the project and that the speaker didn't look anyone in the eye. You suffered from the halo effect because your initial impression overshadowed any other clues that may have been present.

Person Perception

"Everyone makes observations of people's behavior (both other people and ourselves) and draws conclusions about other people's personality traits. People use their knowledge of these traits, and of the effects of various situations, to predict how others will behave. The process by which people make such predictions is called person perception.

75

According to Swann (1984), people are generally poor at making predictions about others' personality traits. People tend to assume that others are consistent in their behavior from situation to situation. They tend to overlook or misperceive evidence that contradicts their own first impressions, and

© Matej Kastelic/Shutterstock.com

they overlook the effects that situations have on people's behavior."*

Identity Cues

"Identity cues include particular styles of clothing or other nonverbal factors (jewelry, hairstyle, body art, etc.) that give others a way to judge identity. If others appear to perceive you in a way that contradicts your own view of yourself, for example, you will tend to show cues designed to change the perception.

© Halfpoint/Shutterstock.com

Think back to the beginning of the chapter to the discussion of selection. These concepts can also be linked to perceptual selectivity in a public speaking situation. It may be difficult for audience members to see their own faults, but can easily magnify the faults perceived in a presenter. For example, if an audience member makes a judgment about you, the presenter, (let's say that you are perceived as being disorganized) that is not consistent with what you believe about yourself (let's say you pride yourself on your organizational skills), you may tend to screen out that information. This creates and reinforces a misleading self-concept. Conversely, you may respond to an audience member given your perception of that person, rather than what the person is really like."*

Stereotyping

"Stereotyping results from over-generalizing or making weak generalizations about people, places, or events. Cultural stereotypes are the tendency to see all members of a particular group of people as having the same characteristics."* Often these cultural stereotypes are unfavorable and put people at an unfair disadvantage.

© Ljupco Smokovski/Shutterstock.com

"Some stereotypes go beyond simply categorizing people according to cultural background, and respond to people's occupations or roles they portray."* For example, public relations professionals are sometimes incorrectly stereotyped as "spin doctors"—those who bend the truth to fit the need of the organization – when, in reality, the public relations profession prides itself on its ethics, professional transparency, and truthfulness in messaging.

"Stereotyping can help you determine how to behave in a particular environment. For example, you might be conscious of the need to behave well in a doctor or lawyer's office because you expect that person to behave a certain way, and you assume that he or she has behavioral expectations of you as well."*

"In general, though, stereotyping can be far more harmful than helpful. At one time or another, most people have held fixed impressions (whether consciously or unconsciously) of others according to a specific ethnic or cultural background, occupation, or perhaps even income level."*

Attribution

Attribution is a significant concept in public relations speaking. When your audience

© Monkey Business Images/Shutterstock.com

views people and situations, it is only natural for them to base their impressions on their perceptual interpretations. "Audience members make sense of things depending on what they already know or think they know about a particular presenter or situation. This can be good in one sense, because they are able to use those impressions to guide their behavior. The audience forms first impressions of others based on physical characteristics and personal attributes. Sometimes audience members have only these superficial things to go by when making a judgment about a speaker and his or her message. Audiences often make judgments about speakers based solely on appearance."* This is why personal appearance and likeability is so important in public speaking, with the latter relating directly to the perceived integrity of a presenter. This is the most important aspect of the presenter's ability to persuade an audience.

If the audience is given a chance to interact with the speaker on a personal level, such as in an interactive workshop-style session or through question-and-answer periods in a press conference-style setting, the audience will enhance their impression by evaluating the speaker's particular personality traits, and they may even be able to pick up on the presenter's beliefs and attitudes. With the goal of not only reaching your audience, but having the audience respond in the manner you wish, it is important to remember that when the audience begins to make guesses about what motivates the speaker, and actually start building a personality for him or her, they have gone beyond simply interpreting what they see and hear in the presentation. At this point they've begun to speculate that they know things about the presenter that they can't actually see.

© Halfpoint/Shutterstock.com

An audience member's first impressions aren't always accurate, but once people form an opinion of someone, they tend to hold on to it and base their future encounters on that initial perception. In an ideal world, an audience could improve their interpretive abilities by being more conscious of how they draw conclusions about first impressions. "A television commercial for a dandruff shampoo helped put the power of first impressions in perspective. In the commercial, the actress suggested to her dandruff-stricken friend that 'You never get a second chance to make a first impression.'"* The same holds true in the practice of public relations.

© racorn/Shutterstock.com

Now let's look at you, the speaker. Typically, two kinds of errors can occur in the attribution process. "The first, the *self-serving bias* happens when we take credit for positive attributions and deny negative ones."* For example, when delivering a presentation, you may coordinate your visual aid well with the oral presentation, which you gladly acknowledge praise and recognition for, but your oral presentation is laced with vocalized pauses (ums and ahs), which you refuse to acknowledge or make efforts to correct.

"The second typical error is *over attribution* in which a person will single out one or two characteristics and attribute everything to those specific characteristics."* Consider the situation where your co-worker may dress too casually for the prescribed office decorum. When you see your co-worker make a mistake on a report and is tardy for work one day, you attribute these mistakes to a casual work ethic symbolized by the casual dress. In reality, the co-worker who made the mistake was just learning the job and happened to have a flat tire on the way to work that day.

© Mehmet Dilsiz/Shutterstock.com

This chapter took a specific look at the perception process from the audience and speaker's perspective. The process of perception plays a key role in establishing relationships with others. By understanding the perceptual process and making a concentrated effort toward increasing perceptual accuracy, presenters can increase their chances for effective message delivery. In the next chapter we will examine the importance of nonverbal behavior in the communication process.

Coach's Corner: Take Perception Seriously

If you are coaching an executive, you must ensure that the executive is aware of how he and/or the company are perceived. Whether or not the executive agrees with the perception of the organization's publics, it is absolutely essential that he understands that it exists and it is your responsibility to guide the executive in achieving that understanding. This can be a difficult task when an ego gets in the way. Together you must develop a strategy to capitalize on the perception if it is a positive perception or to mitigate and eliminate it if it is a negative perception.

© eurobanks/Shutterstock.com

REVIEW TERMS AND CONCEPTS

- ✓ Perception
- ✓ Selection
- ✓ Organization
- ✓ Interpretation
- ✓ Halo effect

- ✓ Person perception
- ✓ Identity cues
- ✓ Stereotyping
- ✓ Attribution

APPLICATION IN ACTION

1. As a public relations speech writer, presenter, and executive coach, it is essential to remember that audience perception of the message and the messenger (whether that is you or your boss) greatly influences the successful delivery and receipt of the message.

© Oilyy/Shutterstock.com

2. Attend a presentation on campus and document the three parts of the sense-making process an audience employs when listening to a presentation, i.e., selection, organization, and interpretation. Present your findings in class.

   I.   Purpose
        A. The purpose of this form of informative presentation is to share your perceptions of a public presentation that you attended.

   II. Objectives
        A. Prepare an informative speech in 1- to 2-page outline following the format of the template and guidelines of the rubric located at the end of this chapter.
        B. Deliver a 3- to 4-minute informative speech (visual aid optional).
        C. Observe informative speeches given by other members of the class.
        D. Practice researching, writing, organizing and speaking skills.
        E. Practice a type of speech you will use later in your professional career (practical application).

   III. Instructions
        A. Attend an on-campus presentation, such as a public lecture, speaker's series, classroom lecture, etc.
        B. Document the three parts of the sense-making process by answering the prompts in the listener perception assignment worksheet sheet that follows.
        C. Create an outline based on the information you will present. **Bring a typed copy of your outline as well as the rubric to class** with your name on it to give to the instructor just prior to presenting your speech.

LISTENER PERCEPTION ASSIGNMENT WORKSHEET

Selection (Individuals in the audience will tend to pay attention to those stimuli that are of interest to them or with which are familiar, based on past experiences.)

1. What aspects of the presentation most interested you and why?

_____

_____

_____

_____

Organization (Individuals in the audience, when presented with ambiguous issues, discuss those issues with other members of their social network, in this case, other audience members.)

2. What in the presentation was ambiguous or confusing and led you to ask, or you wish you would have asked, another audience member to clarify?

_____

_____

_____

_____

Interpretation (Once individuals in an audience have selected and organized sensory data, they need to give that data meaning. Interpretation is giving meaning to that information.)

3. In what manner did you give meaning to the selected information, e.g., past experience, emotional state, or social influence and context?

_____

_____

_____

_____

_____

SPEECH OUTLINE TEMPLATE

Instructions. You will use this template to create the draft of your speech outline.
    1. Remove these two pages from your textbook.
    2. Complete each section using a pencil (this will allow you to easily make changes).
    3. Exchange your completed draft with your speech coach for feedback.
    4. Submit your edited draft to your instructor on the assigned date.

Specific Purpose:

_____

_____

Thesis Statement:

_____

_____

_____

Introduction

    I.   *Attention-getting material:*

    II.   *Establish credibility:*

    III.   *Preview/thematic statement:*

        [Transition: _____.]

Body

    I.   _____
        A.
        B.
        C.

        [Transition: _____.]

(*Body continued*)
II. _____
        A.
        B.
        C.

        [Transition: _____.]

III. _____
        A.
        B.
        C.

        [Transition: _____.]

IV. _____
        A.
        B.
        C.

        [Transition: _____.]

Conclusion

I.   *Summary Statement:*

II.   *Concluding Remarks:*

Bibliography

1.
2.
3.

INFORMATIVE SPEECH EVALUATION RUBRIC (PERCEPTION)

NAME _____	
CONTENT	**DELIVERY**
INTRODUCTION (10 POINTS) • Opening statement that <u>doesn't announce topic</u> (Attention getter) • Establishes credibility • Previews the speech • Thesis Statement	**EYE CONTACT** (10 POINTS) • Directness • Randomness
BODY (15 POINTS) • 1- to 2-page typed outline following the three-level, full-sentence format (no paragraphs), numbering, and general appearance in the textbook • Contains 3 main points in a clear organizational pattern • Major points of the speech are linked together with <u>transitions</u>	**VOICE & MOVEMENT** (10 POINTS) • Projection • Minimal Vocalized Pauses • Posture • Gestures
CONCLUSION (5 POINTS) • Summarizes the main points of the speech • Ends with a quotation, story, or ties back to opening sentence ("clincher")	**TIME** (10 POINTS) • Conformed to 3- to 4-minute time limit
VISUAL AID (NOT GRADED) • Handling of Aid • Appearance	
TIME: **GRADE:**	

Coaching for Informative Speech

Assignment: Remove this page from your text and bring to class on the day that your speaking partner presents their speech. During the presentation, take notes based on the questions provided below. Then, write a one-to two-page critique discussing your answers to those questions as you assess your speaking partner. This should be written in paragraph form.

1. How well did the speaker convey the three aspects of the sense-making process?

2. How effectively did the speaker grab your attention? How well did the conclusion summarize the presentation?

3. Was the speech organized in accordance with the outline template and were transitions used effectively?

4. "Comment on the speaker's voice, gestures, and facial expressions? Were they used appropriately to engage the audience? Was the voice modulated in pitch and volume?"**

Credits:

Nonverbal Communication

© g-stockstudio/Shutterstock.com

Chapter 5

Objectives

At the completion of this chapter you should be able to:

- ✓ Understand the significance of nonverbal behavior as it relates to your audience and to you as a public speaker.

- ✓ Describe the characteristics of nonverbal behavior.

- ✓ Implement a variety of nonverbal tools in your public relations transactions.

- ✓ Demonstrate your ability to analyze nonverbal behaviors observed in a product commercial.

"People have long been aware of the importance of nonverbal communication. Yet how or why nonverbal can be so powerful has remained somewhat of a mystery."* These behaviors that often occur outside the level of a speaker's consciousness can profoundly influence the success or failure of your presentation. How we say something often has more impact than what we are saying. "In this chapter, we want to help you increase your understanding of the significance of nonverbal behavior as

© racorn/Shutterstock.com

part of your total communication package when it comes to public speaking in a public relations context. We'll examine various perspectives, characteristics, and forms of nonverbal behavior, and offer several skills you can master to avoid sending unintentional or incongruent messages."* We'll also offer skills to help develop sensitivity, accuracy and comprehension in *receiving* nonverbal messages from your audience.

NONVERBAL COMMUNICATION

"You've heard them before, those common expressions such as 'actions speak louder than words' or 'a picture is worth a thousand words.' Such is the 'folk wisdom' about the everyday use of, and believability in the power of the nonverbal. Nonverbal simply means 'not words.' The definition of the word nonverbal says, 'It does not pertain to, or is not in the form of words.' Communication professor Judee Burgoon (1989) defines nonverbal communication as 'those attributes or actions of humans, other than the use of words themselves, which have socially shared meaning, are intentionally sent or interpreted as intentional, or consciously sent

or consciously received, and have potential for feedback from the receiver.'"*

Nonverbal communication includes a wide range of phenomena. The way you sit, position your gaze, or place your arms (crossed or not) all communicate something about you. Without using words, your choices of clothing, grooming, and posture consciously or unconsciously communicates to people around you. For example, the President of the United States always wears a suit and tie when delivering the State of the Union

© Rena Schild/Shutterstock.com

address. His apparel not only reflects the seriousness and formality of this annual event, but also

is a conveyance of respect to his audience.

"For purposes of clarification, you can think of nonverbal communication as all aspects

of interaction that influence the messages you get, or seem to get, from another person that do

not involve the spoken word. This can include messages that you send your audience as well as

messages your audience sends to you. These messages may consist of facial expressions, body

movements, vocal qualities, and other associated voice elements. *Nonverbal* phenomena can be

characterized in very different ways from how we characterize *verbal* communication."*

CHARACTERISTICS

"Nonverbal signals are ongoing, visible, and often difficult to manipulate or conceal."*

Whether you try to send a signal or you stay silent with a neutral expression on your face, a

receiver still interprets your uninterrupted stream of behavior. The receiver may interpret this

expression as boredom or disinterest. College professors frequently observe this behavior in student during class sessions. The student attempts to appear interested by looking at the lecturing professor when, in reality, this neutral expression is interpreted by the professor as a lack of interest. The communication takes place in the reception and interpretation of the message.

Nonverbal communication is ambiguous and is the primary mode of expressing emotion. These concepts are especially relevant to the public relations speaker—particularly involving a crisis

© Picsfive/Shutterstock.com

situation—because, in addition to sending verbal messages, the speaker sends nonverbal messages to the audience who, in turn, assigns meaning to those nonverbal messages. Recall that the CEO of a major airline gave his first media briefing within minutes after one of their aircraft crash landed in a New York river. The CEO's nonverbal communication—voice projection, voice tenor, posture, eye contact, gestures, and professional attire—conveyed an impression of confidence, clarity, and control—which is just what is needed in a time of crisis—to the media and other publics, such as the families of passengers.

Interestingly, "psychologist Albert Mehrabian concluded that as little as 7 percent of the emotional

> **Perception is Reality**
>
> A Latin saying, *Vestis virum reddit,* means "The clothes make the man." Gender specificity aside, it is important to dress for success when making your speech. When you dress professionally, you will be perceived by your audience as prepared, knowledgeable, and organized. This nonverbal communication tactic will further enhance your credibility as a speaker.

meaning of a message is communicated through explicit verbal channels. Our face communicates 55% of the meaning and vocal cues communicate 38%. This means that 93% of emotional meaning happens nonverbally."* Therefore, those nonverbal cues that the speaker gives to the audience can help or hinder the delivery and successful reception of the message.

Nonverbal messages can mean several things, depending on such factors as context, culture, and personality. Some people get very quiet when they're happy. Others express happiness through smiles, shouts for joy, and even tears. You need to remember the factors of context such as the surrounding events in which your audience is receiving the message, to have any success at understanding your audience's nonverbal signals.

"Nonverbal messages are more believable than the spoken word in both interpersonal and public speaking contexts. We tend to believe what we perceive in nonverbal messages. As mentioned earlier in this chapter, the expression "Actions speak louder than words," supports this idea. Why is that? To some extent, our nonverbal behavior comes from a portion of the brain that is more instinctual and therefore harder to mask. When an audience receives mixed verbal and nonverbal messages, the audience tends to believe the nonverbal content more than the verbal."* If a speaker conveys a stoic demeanor yet states how enthusiastic he or she is to be speaking at an event, the audience will likely doubt his or her sincerity because the facial expression doesn't match the verbal message. In the next section, we'll discuss how to avoid situations such as this by utilizing a variety of nonverbal tools.

NONVERBAL TOOLS

You communicate nonverbally through the tools in your communication package. Although you are born with capacity to

communicate, it is the development and use of these tools that enables you to successfully deliver and interpret nonverbal messages. The first tool we'll explore is paralinguistics.

Paralinguistics

"Paralinguistics or paralanguage means 'with language' or 'accompanying speech.' Perhaps an easy way to understand paralanguage is by thinking about not *what* you are saying, but *how* you are saying it. If you say, 'How are you today?' with the emphasis on 'How' or 'How are you today?' with the emphasis on 'today,' you have changed the meaning of the question through your tone and inflection.

Paralanguage can include laughing, crying, tsking, sighing, as well as pitch, articulation, rhythm, resonance, tempo, volume, yelling, whispering, moaning, whining, and yawning. Of importance to the public relations speaker, it also includes vocalized pauses (noises made to take the place of words) such as 'uh,' 'Uh-huh,' 'uh uh,' 'shhh,' and other clicks, snorts, and sniffs."* Other physical features, such as facial expression and body posture have a mediating effect on the message your voice projects. "For example, if you sound irritated but you're smiling, your listener may get a mixed message. If you're smiling, your vocal tone is friendly, and your body looks relaxed, your listener is getting a consistent message rather than a contradictory one. The tone and inflection of your voice, in itself, carries a message."* An awareness of all the nonverbal and verbal messages you transmit at any given moment can help make you a better public speaker.

Eye Behavior

One of the most important aspects of public speaking involves eye behavior. "Have you ever heard the expression 'Your eyes are the windows to your soul'? Or, perhaps you've heard of someone giving 'the evil eye.' Eyes are powerful signaling devices. When the eyes of two people meet, there is a special kind of communication."* The term eye contact is often used to describe this kind of visual

© racorn/Shutterstock.com

interaction in public speaking. "Whether or not to look someone straight in the eye, and for how long, is a product of your culture and the context of your encounter. In public speaking, satisfactory eye contact with your audience is measured in terms of positive eye contact and occurs when maintaining eye contact with your audience for at least 75 percent of your presentation.

On the other hand, gaze avoidance can also be meaningful and indicate psychological distance, insincerity, or even shame. Gaze aversion refers to the practice, common among people in a normal conversation, of looking at the speaker or receiver at times and at other times looking away. On the individual level, in many cultures it's considered a sign of respect to avoid eye contact with someone

© rangizzz/Shutterstock.com

who is older or more important than you are. In fact, even in mainstream culture of the United States, a direct stare is considered a social offense to be avoided. The stare can be interpreted as an invasion of someone's privacy, or even as a threatening gesture, commonly referred to as a 'predatory gaze.'"* This is important for the public speaker or executive coach to remember when the speaker is addressing members of another culture where direct eye contact would be considered offensive.

Body Movement

Psychologists Paul Ekman and William Friesen (1975) believed there are five types of body expressions: (1) emblems, (2) illustrators, (3) regulators, (4) affect displays, and (5) adaptors. All are applicable in the public speaking realm.

Emblems are usually gestural equivalents of a word or phrase. For example, the phrase 'Come here' can easily be replaced by the familiar motion of bringing the open hand and arm toward the chest in a repeated motion. The 'peace' or 'victory' sign made with the fingers are also examples of emblems. Emblematic movements most frequently occur when the verbal channel is blocked. Let's say a speaker enters a room

© Asier Romero/Shutterstock.com

to an audience's standing ovation and loud applause. She waves to the audience as a gesture of appreciation since her voice wouldn't be audible over the background noise. Conversely, the raised arm with open palm may be used to quell hostile shouts from an angry audience.

The referent for many emblems is purely arbitrary. Twirling the forefinger around near your temple to indicate that your opponent across the stage in a political campaign debate is insane has no visual connection with the concept of madness, or with the acts of the insane. Emblems, like language, are learned in everyday social

© moshimochi/Shutterstock.com

99

interaction and, for the most part are culturally specific. For example, the American use of the forefinger and thumb placed together to make the 'OK' sign is considered to be an obscene gesture in some cultures.

Illustrators are directly linked to speech because these actions illustrate what is being said orally, and, for the most part, are intentional acts. People speak rhythmically, and also gesture in time to vocalizations. A gesture can add emphasis to a particular part of a phrase when speaking to a group. Illustrators also express logical relations or directions and special relationships. In fact, in difficult communication situations—such as describing the size and shape of something—people tend to use more illustrators and are frustrated in certain situations

where they can't be used—when talking on the phone, for example (Rutter, 1986). Illustrators are also movements in which people point to an object to which they are verbally referring. Some illustrators—acts that designate or depict—can stand alone, without verbal support."* For example, the

© Champion studio/Shutterstock.com

index finger pressed to the lips means the same thing as a vocalized "shhhh" and tells the audience to be quiet. However, other illustrators—those emphasizing rhythm or relationship—can only be understood in the verbal message. The open-hands gesture illustrated above is meaningless without an accompanying verbal description to establish the relationship.

"Regulators are actions that serve to control oral interaction between two or more people."* They tell the public speaker such things as repeat, elaborate, or speed up. "An example of a common regulator witnessed by a public speaker in his audience is head nods for 'Keep

going.' Most regulators, like illustrators, can't be understood apart from the verbal messages being exchanged. Leaning forward or backward, indicative of an audience's interest in your topic, breaking eye contact, and the raising of eyebrows can all be classified as regulators.

Affect displays are body expressions that reflect the emotional state of the communicator. Because facial expressions are the principal way most humans convey their feelings, a face that shows anger, fear, or disgust is displaying an affective state. Like the body movements discussed in the previous categories, affect displays are not tightly bound to verbal expressions. Furthermore, affect displays tend to be less consciously controllable than the previous types. For example, people often seem

© Paul Matthew Photography /Shutterstock.com

to know how others feel, or ask 'What's wrong?' because of affect displays they observe. However, because people often try to manage the impressions others have of them, people try to mask their own affect displays. Examples include you masking your exhaustion or anxiety when having to present to a group. Someone else might mask hurt at an insult or joy at being dealt a good hand in poker. In fact, the term 'poker face' has been coined for not letting emotions show in a card game or in any social context such as public speaking. Think of the times people have read *your* affect displays.

Adaptors are movements, learned in childhood, that are part of a patterned activity. Adaptors are more difficult to define and are open

© NattapolStudiO/Shutterstock.com

101

to more speculation than most other gestures. There are three types of adaptors: (1) self-adaptors, such as hair brushing, remnants of a learned activity toward one's own body; (2) alter (stress) adaptors, or movements learned in the process of interpersonal relation such as the restless movement of hands and feet, because of anxiety; and, (3) object-adaptors, such as using a tool like a pencil. Each of these kinds of adaptor movements is performed without one's awareness. The good news is that they are not generally noticed or commented on by others.

Artifactual Communication

Artifactual communication includes all those artifacts or elements that you add to your body, such as earrings (how many, where placed, how long), watches, necklaces, eyeglasses (how long you spend at an optometrist's mirror until you find the frames that are "you"), hairpieces, wigs, eyeliners,

© Minerva Studio/Shutterstock.com

perfumes, and other cosmetic devices. Other artifacts that act as extensions of self can include the car you drive, the way you decorate your house, or the designer jeans or athletic shoes you wear. These extensions act as nonverbal status symbols."*

In this chapter, you've hopefully gained a clearer understanding of the significance of nonverbal behavior as it relates to your audience and to you as a public speaker. You've examined various characteristics and forms of nonverbal behavior. Nonverbal competence pays a high reward in avoiding misunderstandings and enhancing your credibility and message effectiveness with your audience. Now that you understand the importance of nonverbal behavior in the context of public relations public speaking, the next chapter will look closely at the considerations necessary in delivering a polished presentation.

Coach's Corner: Seeking Feedback

Encourage those executives that you coach to seek feedback from others about the nonverbal messages that they send as a matter of routine and in a formal presentation situations. By seeking feedback from you and others, their nonverbal competence will increase to the point that they will not make many nonverbal "slips."

© eurobanks/Shutterstock.com

REVIEW TERMS AND CONCEPTS

- ✓ Nonverbal communication
- ✓ Characteristics
- ✓ Ambiguous
- ✓ Emotional meaning
- ✓ Paralinguistics
- ✓ Eye behavior
- ✓ Body movement

- ✓ Emblems
- ✓ Illustrators
- ✓ Regulators
- ✓ Affect displays
- ✓ Adaptors
- ✓ Artifactual communication

APPLICATION IN ACTION

1. Nonverbal behaviors often occur outside the level of a speaker's consciousness and can profoundly influence the success or failure of a presentation. *How* something is said often has more impact than *what* is actually being said.

© Oilyy/Shutterstock.com

2. The public relations profession commonly partners with an organization's advertising and marketing functions in an integrated marketing communication role. Watch a product commercial on the web or on television and document the actors' nonverbal behavior using the nonverbal communication assignment worksheet that follows. Create and deliver an informative speech describing your findings. Be sure to include the video clip of the commercial that you are analyzing as your visual aid. Present your findings in class.

I.   Purpose
   - A. The purpose of this form of informative presentation is to discuss your analysis of the nonverbal behaviors you observed in a product commercial on the web or on television.

II.   Objectives
   - A. Prepare an informative speech in 1- to 2-page outline following the format of the template and guidelines of the rubric located at the end of this chapter.
   - B. Deliver a 4- to 6-minute informative speech that includes viewing of the video clip.
   - C. Observe informative speeches given by other members of the class.
   - D. Practice researching, writing, organizing and speaking skills.
   - E. Practice a type of speech you will use later in your professional career (practical application!)

III.   Instructions
   - A. Watch a product commercial on the web or on television.
   - B. Document the actors' nonverbal behavior using the nonverbal communication assignment worksheet that follows.

C. Create an outline based on the information you will present. **<u>Bring a typed copy of your outline as well as the rubric to class</u>** with your name on it to give to the instructor just prior to presenting your speech.

NONVERBAL COMMUNICATION ASSIGNMENT WORKSHEET

Paralinguistics (The tone and inflection of your voice, in itself, carries a message: think about *how*, not *what*, they are saying.)

1. What are some examples of the speaker's changes in tone and inflection? Did the speaker's words match his or her voice tone?

_____

_____

_____

_____

Body Movement (All types of body movement are relevant in the public speaking realm.)

2. How did the speaker utilize body movement such as emblems, illustrators, regulators, and affect displays?

_____

_____

_____

_____

Artifactual Communication (Includes all those artifacts or elements that you add to your body, such as earrings, watches, necklaces, eyeglasses, etc.)

3. What appearance cues add to or detract from the effectiveness of the overall message?

_____

_____

_____

_____

SPEECH OUTLINE TEMPLATE

Instructions. You will use this template to create the draft of your speech outline.

    1. Remove these two pages from your textbook.
    2. Complete each section using a pencil (this will allow you to easily make changes).
    3. Exchange your completed draft with your speech coach for feedback.
    4. Submit your edited draft to your instructor on the assigned date.

Specific Purpose:

_____

_____

Thesis Statement:

_____

_____

_____

Introduction

    I.   *Attention-getting material:*

    II.   *Establish credibility:*

    III.   *Preview/thematic statement:*

        [Transition: _____.]

Body

    I.   _____
        A.
        B.
        C.

        [Transition: _____.]

(Body continued)

II. _____

      A.

      B.

      C.

      [Transition: _____ .]

III. _____

      A.

      B.

      C.

      [Transition: _____ .]

IV. _____

      A.

      B.

      C.

      [Transition: _____ .]

Conclusion

I.   *Summary Statement:*

II.   *Concluding Remarks:*

Bibliography

1.

2.

3.

INFORMATIVE SPEECH EVALUATION RUBRIC (NONVERBAL)

NAME _____	

CONTENT	DELIVERY
INTRODUCTION (10 POINTS) • Opening statement that <u>doesn't announce topic</u> (Attention getter) • Establishes credibility • Previews the speech • Thesis Statement	**EYE CONTACT** (10 POINTS) • Directness • Randomness
BODY (15 POINTS) • 1- to 2-page typed outline following the three-level, full-sentence format (no paragraphs), numbering, and general appearance in the textbook • Contains 3 main points in a clear organizational pattern • Major points of the speech are linked with <u>transitions</u>	**VOICE & MOVEMENT** (10 POINTS) • Projection • Minimal Vocalized Pauses • Posture • Gestures
CONCLUSION (5 POINTS) • Summarizes the main points of the speech • Ends with a quotation, story, or ties back to opening sentence ("clincher")	**TIME** (10 POINTS) • Conformed to 4- to 6-minute time limit
VISUAL AID (5) • Handling of Aid • Appearance	

TIME:	GRADE:	

Coaching for Informative Speech

Assignment: Remove this page from your text and bring to class on the day that your speaking partner presents their speech. During the presentation, take notes based on the questions provided below. Then, write a one- to two-page critique discussing your answers to those questions as you assess your speaking partner. This should be written in paragraph form.

1. How well did the speaker document the nonverbal behaviors observed in the commercial?

2. Describe how the speaker incorporated the video clip into the presentation. Was it effective?

3. How effectively did the speaker grab your attention? How well did the conclusion summarize the presentation?

4. Was the speech organized in accordance with the outline template and were transitions used effectively?

5. Comment on the speaker's voice, gestures, and facial expressions? Were they used appropriately to engage the audience? How well did the speaker incorporate pauses to avoid filler words?

Credits:

Delivering the Presentation

© Denniro/Shutterstock.com

Objectives

At the completion of this chapter you should be able to:

✓ Analyze your audience and speaking environment.

✓ Show the importance of using your voice and eye contact to your advantage.

✓ Incorporate gestures and movement in your public relations presentations.

✓ Demonstrate your ability to incorporate key delivery considerations in the form of a eulogy.

In the previous two chapters you have learned about the important connections between verbal and nonverbal communication for the public relations speaker. By the time you finish this chapter, you should be able to analyze your audience and speaking environment, demonstrate the importance of using your voice and eye contact to your advantage, as well as comfortably incorporate gestures and movement in your presentations. These important delivery considerations can make the difference between a speech that bores and a speech that wows! Let's begin with audience analysis.

© Rawpixel/Shutterstock.com

AUDIENCE ANALYSIS

When you plan a presentation you must consider your audience first and foremost. While there may be rare occasions when a corporate spokesperson does not have the luxury of conducting a thorough audience analysis, in most cases a corporate speech writer must analyze the audience in advance in order to effectively convey the message.

Compare the public speaking situation to any other type of interpersonal exchange in which you size up the individual (or individuals) with whom you are speaking. In essence, you are analyzing your audience. Imagine you are planning a conversation in which you are going to ask someone to do something for you that might be rather difficult. You will consider what time of day is best to approach this person, how much time you have to convey your request, and how you will adapt your word choice to the situation. In a similar vein, planning a speech involves knowing your audience's attitudes and motives for listening in addition to their demographics. You must analyze all of the factors that come into play: time, place, topic, and audience.

You must first consider the purpose of your presentation. Is this a speech promoting goodwill or is this a speech in response to a crisis that an organization or a public figure is facing? Next, when analyzing their audiences, speech writers must consider the background of their audience and their

© Pressmaster/Shutterstock.com

knowledge (or lack thereof) of the topic. Is this a friendly audience that will be in close agreement with what you are saying, or is this a hostile audience that you will attempt to persuade to shift their opinion of a given situation? For example, if you are representing a nonprofit organization that advocates for the abolition of the death penalty, and three quarters of your audience are strongly against your position, you stand little chance of turning them around in the short time you have to give the speech. "If, on the other hand, your audience slightly favors, or is at least neutral toward your position, you have a better chance of persuading."*

Before your audience will buy into *what* you are saying, they need to buy into *you.* This means that the more you can demonstrate to your audience that you are like them, the more likely you are to successfully connect with them. Think back to some of the most effective speakers you've heard. What did they have in common? They certainly came across as capable in their delivery, they were knowledgeable, and they were likable. These three attributes resulted in the audience believing in what they said and thereby believing in the organization and position they represented. In essence, the speaker and audience bonded.

Finally, we would be remiss if we didn't discuss how the use of humor should factor into your audience analysis. We discourage the use of humor in presentations in most cases. Consider that in our diverse business world, some forms of humor can be perceived as offensive or inappropriate as it relates to gender, race or culture. Do not use humor if it doesn't come naturally to you. Forced humor can be awkward for both the speaker and the audience. However, in limited instances humor can be effective if tasteful and *appropriate*

© Monkey Business Images/Shutterstock.com

for the topic and the occasion. Instead, the use of an inspirational story or quotation is for more affective in enhancing your message.

In this section we addressed the various aspects of audience analysis. As much as you can, do your homework before you present. Often you will be in contact with the person representing the organization or group that has asked you to speak and it is likely that he or she have some specific expectations about the outcome of your presentation or the presentation you are writing for someone else. Ask the contact person to give you as much information as possible about the audience and expectations ahead of time. After all, both you and the contact person have a lot at stake. Now let's look at various physical aspects of delivery.

VOCAL CONSIDERATIONS

Having analyzed your audience and written your speech, it's now time to rehearse your presentation. We recommend that you practice your presentation out loud. A speech sounds very different when we simply silently read through it. We may think we are rehearsing variations in rate, tone, pitch, etc., but it is not the same as actually speaking out loud. Novice speakers are often surprised when they rehearse what they think is a five-minute presentation and find out after they have delivered the speech that it was just under four minutes! Remember, public speaking is both a psychological and physical action and this is why you need to vocalize what you have written. Now let's examine the various components of vocalizing your presentation.

Rate

You will recall from chapter one that anxiety is usually at its highest at the beginning of your speech, and can lead to speaking faster than you anticipate. The goal is to speak at a controlled rate. More often than not, you should speak even slower than you think you

© Larry Rains/Shutterstock.com

need to. By doing so, you will most likely speak at a rate that your audience can follow and comprehend. If you speak too quickly, your audience misses much of what you are saying as your words will sound jumbled. If you speak too slowly, you will lose your audience's attention. While we encourage a controlled rate of speaking, we also note that effective speakers will vary their rate for the purposes of emphasis throughout their presentation. A politician campaigning for office and speaking before a large crowd may purposely slow her rate dramatically when making an important point. This action signals to the audience that what she is saying is so important that it needs to be emphasized and listened to very carefully.

On the other hand, if a speaker is trying to convey excitement or urgency, she might temporarily speed up the message to recapture the audience's attention. Let's say you represent a charitable organization that serves the medical needs of wounded members of the armed forces. Your purpose is to raise money for the organization because there is now a surge of wounded warriors who are in need of your organization's assistance. You can express this sense of urgency on this particular point by increasing the rate of your presentation to ensure audience attention.

Tone

In addition to varying our rate, fluctuations in tone also enhance speaker effectiveness. The goal is to have a polished, conversational style of speaking. When you have a conversation with someone, you naturally vary your tone. Effective speakers who strive for a conversational style of delivery are far more effective than speakers who stick to a script and read word-for-word. There's nothing worse than sitting through a monotone presentation. Many of us recall the famous clip from the movie *Ferris Bueller's Day*

© g-stockstudio/Shutterstock.com

Off, where the teacher has been painfully droning on and on and is attempting to gain some class participation—"Anyone? Anyone?"

Have your tone match your message. The more serious your message, the more serious your tone should be. Recall from the previous chapter, if you are speaking about a light-hearted topic and your tone is somber, you will lose credibility, as your nonverbal message does not match the spirit of the presentation. Unintentional variations in tone can result from nervousness as well. It all goes back to rehearsing out loud.

Volume

We know that varying our rate and tone leads to greater engagement with our audience. But did you know that changing your volume is effective as well? Sometimes speaking very softly, almost whispering, can draw your audience in as effectively as speaking loudly. It can be a very smart attention-drawing technique. It says, "Listen closely to what I am saying," or "Shhh….I only want this particular audience to hear what I am saying." Conversely, surprising your audience with an unexpected increase in volume can have a similar affect. As with rate and tone, you want to seek a balanced level of volume.

The acoustics of the room in which you are speaking will also influence how loudly or quietly you will need to project your voice. If you will be speaking with a microphone you will definitely want to test the sound system ahead of time so you aren't the speaker who starts out by saying, "Can everyone hear me?" This goes back to checking out your speaking environment ahead of time. Preparation is key.

Vocalized Pauses

Vocalized pauses are fancy words for filler words. We all have heard them—um, uh, and-uh, err, like, and you know. The words "you know" are often inserted for a variety of reasons, one of which is simply habit. The speaker is not feeling confident and wants to get some feedback from their audience. The question "you know?" is actually asking the audience if they are following what the speaker is saying.

Perception is Reality
Novice speakers are often very uncomfortable when they experience a pause in their presentation. Maybe they need to find their place in their notes, or they have momentarily drawn a blank. More often than not, the audience is not even aware. As a matter of fact, most audiences appreciate a moment of pause so they can process what they have just heard. Furthermore, the speaker who is comfortable with pauses is actually perceived by the audience as more confident. The pause says to the listeners, "What I just said was important, and I want you to think about it for a second." While some speakers may feel uncomfortable with pauses, effective speakers use pauses for additional emphasis and overall effectiveness.

Speakers fill a void by plugging in these fillers—also known as non-fluencies—when they are searching for their next thought. Unfortunately, many speakers are not even aware that they use fillers until it is pointed out by a teacher or speaking coach. A short pause may feel like an eternity to the speaker, but the audience may not even notice. They notice when you add the filler word. The more comfortable the speaker is with pausing, the less likely he or she is to fill the void with distracting and meaningless sounds. Now that we have discussed various vocal considerations, let's look at eye contact, one of the most important aspects of delivery.

EYE CONTACT

Eye contact, or lack thereof, can make or break a presentation. Do you really have to look directly at your audience when delivering a speech? The answer is YES! There is an old myth that suggests that if you look just above your audience's heads they will think that you are looking at them. This couldn't be further from the truth. Do you really trust someone who won't look you in the eye?

Speakers who avoid making eye contact lose credibility. The speaker who looks down or away from the audience comes across as inauthentic and insincere. The fact is that eye contact

© doglikehorse/Shutterstock.com

connects you with the audience and maintains their attention. How will you know how your message is being received if you don't look at your audience and see their reactions? If see that your audience is nodding in agreement, you can continue your message with even more confidence than you had when you began. On the other hand, if people are looking perplexed, that may be your signal to elaborate more on the particular subject or provide a more concrete example of what you are explaining. Insecurity may cause you to rely too heavily on your notes and thereby reduce your eye contact with your audience. For some, it is more comfortable to keep looking at their notes than to make direct eye contact. By the way, brief glances up from looking at your notes do not constitute eye contact. In the previous chapter we asserted that you should strive for maintaining eye contact with your audience for at least 75 percent of the presentation. Additionally, recall in Chapter 1 where we suggested that when you first get up in front of your audience, you should take a moment and look around the room, smile, and make eye contact as a means of reducing speaker anxiety. See who smiles back and make sure you first look at them when you start speaking. Once you become more comfortable, broaden your scan of the audience.

When making direct eye contact, pause your gaze for a moment before you look at another person or in another direction. This is easy when the group is smaller. For larger audiences, you will want to look at groups or sections of people rather than trying to make

© Sergey Nivens/Shutterstock.com

direct eye contact with each individual. Furthermore, the effective speaker will look at their audience more than they will look at their notes or visuals. Chapter 2 gave you plenty of tips on the use of visuals, but we want to remind you here that your eye contact should not be fixed on your visual aid projected on the big screen next to you or behind you. Trust what is on the screen and instead focus on your audience. Direct eye contact speaks volumes.

GESTURES AND MOVEMENT

You've prepared your speech and as you begin to rehearse you might be wondering, what do I do with my hands and my feet? In this next section we'll explore appropriate gestures and movements to further enhance your verbal presentation effectiveness.

Gestures

Gestures, when used appropriately, should reinforce the speaker's message. Most people gesture naturally in normal conversation. Since we advocate a polished, conversational delivery, it would make sense to include natural gestures in your presentations. For example, when listing things for your audience, you might use your fingers to support your listing of one, two, and three by showing one, two, and three fingers. Or, if you are

© Thodoris Tibilis/Shutterstock.com

describing the magnitude of an issue you might spread your arms out wide, indicating that it is really big.

Gestures should be controlled and purposeful. Some speakers pick up annoying habits that they aren't even aware of. Playing with one's hair or watch, or jingling change in a pocket, can be very distracting to the audience. As a matter of fact, when speakers use their hands in ways that do not support their message, the

© wavebreakmedia/Shutterstock.com

audience will often start to focus on the distracting gestures rather than the speaker's message.

Having your hands out and open in front of you and above your waist portrays a sense of openness. Try to keep your gestures smooth and fluid, not fast and jerky. The bigger the audience, the more distinct your gestures should be. You want them to be seen. Vary your gestures so they do not become predictable but instead appear spontaneous. Use care not to stifle your natural gestures (such as stiffly holding your arms to your side) or you will appear "robotic" to your audience. Do not intimidate your audience by pointing your index finger at them or shaking your fist. Avoid making gestures that make you look nervous or defensive such as crossing your arms in front of you. And finally, if you are using a lectern or podium, do not use a "death grip" and cling to the sides as if your life depended on it.

Movement

If you are speaking directly into a microphone attached to a podium during your presentation, then moving about is not an option. However, there are environments when movement is appropriate. In smaller settings, or when you have a cordless microphone, you may find that some natural movement can work in tandem with your message. Movement should be naturally motivated, not stiff or contrived. Movement should also be used in moderation; too much can be distracting and become the sole focus of your audience. Constant moving or pacing detracts from your credibility as it makes you appear nervous. When you are in a setting that will allow you to move during your presentation, make your movement subtle, perhaps at points of transition. Consider the following example: You are transitioning to a new topic during a presentation on job hunting. You might say, "Now that we have discussed the consequences of lying on your resume, let's move on and talk about the proper ways to cite your experience." As you say this, you would actually take a couple of steps. That way you are verbally *and* physically transitioning. Additionally, moving forward toward your audience and pausing in that spot for a while helps you connect with your audience. By getting up close and personal, you increase the likelihood that the audience will buy into or agree with what you are saying.

RESPECT

Finally, we would be remiss if we didn't address the notion of respect when delivering a presentation. Often overlooked, your conveyance of respect to your audience is a key component of successful public speaking. This means honor the time limits of your presentation, *especially* if there are other speakers. Essentially, your

© Sarah Cheriton-Jones/Shutterstock.com

allotted time for your presentation is an implicit contract that you make with your audience. If you exceed your time limit, you have broken that contract. Furthermore, if there are a number of speakers scheduled to present and you exceed your allotted time, it is likely the subsequent presenters will feel obligated to cut their presentations short. In this case, you have disrespected both your audience and the other speakers. After some experience, most speakers know their own tendencies and should plan their presentations paying close attention to the mandated time limits.

This chapter has discussed a variety of delivery considerations. Careful and thorough audience analysis will help you adapt your material to that particular audience. Both during rehearsals and during your actual presentations you want to make sure you have consistent eye contact, conversational vocal variation, and appropriate gestures and movement. All of these elements will combine to make your presentation that much more dynamic and effective. In the next chapter we will explore your role as executive speech writer and coach, and extend your understanding of the importance of stagecraft.

Videotaping yourself or the person you are speech coaching can be very useful for reinforcing things that you or the speaker are doing well, in addition to catching things you would not have been aware of had you not actually seen or heard what was happening. For example, if a PR spokesperson for a large corporation was issuing a public apology for a faulty product and he nervously played with his pen the entire time he was speaking and never looked at the audience (or camera), his audience might doubt the authenticity or credibility of the message. On the other hand, if you are coaching a political candidate who complains to you about how nervous she is after each campaign speech, the candidate might be relieved to learn, after watching herself on tape, that she did not *appear* or *sound* nervous at all.

© eurobanks/Shutterstock.com

REVIEW TERMS AND CONCEPTS

✓ Audience analysis

✓ Vocal considerations

✓ Rate

✓ Tone

✓ Volume

✓ Vocalized pauses

✓ Eye contact

✓ Gestures

✓ Movement

✓ Respect

APPLICATION IN ACTION

1. Important delivery considerations can make the difference between a speech that bores and a speech that wows! Analyze your audience and speaking environment, use your voice and eye contact to your advantage, and comfortably incorporate gestures and movement in your presentations.

© Oilyy/Shutterstock.com

2. A eulogy is the most personal form of public speaking. Practice putting together all of the delivery considerations you've just learned about by creating and delivering a eulogy for a deceased celebrity.

I. Purpose
  A. The primary purpose of a eulogy is to say something good about the deceased and give hope to the mourning community.

II. Objectives
  A. Prepare a eulogy in a 1- to 2-page outline following the format of the template and guidelines of the rubric located at the end of this chapter.
  B. Deliver a 3- to 4-minute eulogy for a deceased celebrity from an outline using an electronic visual aid.
  C. Observe eulogies given by other members of the class.
  D. Practice researching, writing, organizing and speaking skills.
  E. Practice a type of speech you may use later in your professional career (practical application).

III. Instructions
  A. You are the public relations spokesperson for a celebrity who has passed away. The celebrity can be a historical figure, politician, professional athlete, or Hollywood actor/actress who is worthy of significant praise.
  B. Library/Internet research is required for this speech. You must have at least 3 sources listed in your bibliography at the end of your outline.
  C. Create an outline based on the information you will present. Bring a typed copy of your outline as well as the rubric to class with your name on it to give to the instructor just prior to presenting your speech.

SPEECH OUTLINE TEMPLATE

Instructions. You will use this template to create the draft of your speech outline.
    1. Remove these two pages from your textbook.
    2. Complete each section using a pencil (this will allow you to easily make changes).
    3. Exchange your completed draft with your speech coach for feedback.
    4. Submit your edited draft to your instructor on the assigned date.

Specific Purpose:

_____

_____

Thesis Statement:

_____

_____

_____

Introduction

    I.   *Attention-getting material:*

    II.   *Establish credibility:*

    III.   *Preview/thematic statement:*

       [Transition: _____.]

Body

    I.   _____
        A.
        B.
        C.

       [Transition: _____.]

(Body continued)

II. _____

        A.

        B.

        C.

        [Transition: _____ .]

III. _____

        A.

        B.

        C.

        [Transition: _____ .]

IV. _____

        A.

        B.

        C.

        [Transition: _____ .]

Conclusion

I.   *Summary Statement:*

II.   *Concluding Remarks:*

Bibliography

1.

2.

3.

EULOGY SPEECH EVALUATION RUBRIC

NAME _____	
CONTENT	**DELIVERY**
INTRODUCTION (10 POINTS) • Opening statement that <u>doesn't announce topic</u> (Attention getter) • Establishes credibility • Previews the speech • Thesis Statement	**EYE CONTACT** (10 POINTS) • Directness • Randomness
BODY (10 POINTS) • 1- to 2-page typewritten outline following the three-level, full-sentence format (no paragraphs), numbering, and general appearance in the textbook • Contains supporting material that sheds a positive light on the deceased celebrity • Major points of the speech are linked with <u>transitions</u>	**VOICE & MOVEMENT** (5 POINTS) • Projection • Minimal Vocalized Pauses • Posture • Gestures
CONCLUSION (5 POINTS) • Summarizes the main points of the speech • Ends with a quotation, story, or ties back to opening sentence ("clincher")	**TIME** (10 POINTS) • Conformed to 3- to 4-minute time limit
VISUAL AID (10 POINTS) • Handling of Aid • Appearance	
TIME: **GRADE:**	

Coaching for Eulogy for a Celebrity Speech

Assignment: Remove this page from your text and bring to class on the day that your speaking partner presents their speech. During the presentation, take notes based on the questions provided below. Then, write a one- to two-page critique discussing your answers to those questions as you assess your speaking partner. This should be written in paragraph form.

1. Did the speaker pick a celebrity that was worthy of praise?

2. What material was included to put the deceased in a positive light?

3. "Comment on the speaker's voice, gestures, and facial expressions? Were they used appropriately to speak to an audience at a memorial service or funeral? Was the voice modulated in pitch and volume?"**

4. How well did the speaker use visuals? Did the speaker maintain eye contact while using visual?

Credits:

*From *Communicating Effectively: Linking Thought and Expression* by Caputo et al. Copyright © 2002 by Kendall Hunt Publishing Company. Reprinted by permission.

**Toastmasters *Advanced Communication Series Public Relations*

Executive Speech Writing and Coaching

Chapter 7

© Stuart Jenner/Shutterstock.com

Objectives

At the completion of this chapter you should be able to:

- ✓ Describe the role of the executive speech writer.

- ✓ Explain the purpose in the preparation of a presentation.

- ✓ Understand the importance of the executive coach's responsibilities with regard to rehearsal and stagecraft.

- ✓ Demonstrate your competency as a speech writer by writing a persuasive speech to be delivered by someone else.

While much of what this book has covered thus far pertains to you, the speaker and/or the speech writer, this chapter will focus on your role as executive speech writer and coach, as well as on stagecraft considerations. How can you help your boss, your CEO, political candidate, or corporate spokesperson project a positive image and represent the organization or constituencies in the best possible light?

THE SPEECH WRITER'S ROLE

For many corporate executives, politicians, organizational leaders, including celebrities such as athletes, public presentations are a fact of life. These individuals may give presentations either occasionally or at multiple events in a single day. Since delivering speeches is

© Khakimullin Aleksandr/Shutterstock.com

not their only job, they often rely on professional speech writers to craft their presentations for them. Similarly, not all professional speech writers spend their entire workdays writing speeches. Often the public affairs or corporate communications specialist may be assigned the task of speech writing in addition to his or her regular duties. Ideally, when asked to write a presentation, he or she will have the luxury of spending an adequate amount of time in preparation.

Speech writers often work for large companies or public figures such as political candidates or government officials. Frequently, former public relations professionals who are good writers become corporate speech writers. Many large corporations employ teams of speech writers to write hundreds of speeches each year. Speech writers may work exclusively for one executive, or they may do freelance speech writing for several executives at a time. When speech writers work exclusively for one person they might be working on several presentations simultaneously. Therefore, they need to be flexible, yet deadline driven. Speech writers come from a variety of academic

© dean bertoncelj/Shutterstock.com

disciplines such as English, journalism, communications, public relations, or professional backgrounds such as politics. Regardless of their background, they need to be excellent writers and have the flexibility to adapt to the varying needs of clients and employers. For example, you may have to provide the talking points for an announcement by your CEO at an initial press conference announcing a product recall, and then help the Human Resources Director craft a message to employees outlining a forthcoming layoff in the organization. In this case, you have two internal clients, the CEO speaking to an external audience (customers) and the Human Resources Director speaking to an internal audience (employees).

For the most part, as a professional speech writer you will not get public credit for your work. You are the ghostwriter behind such figures as the President of the United States or the latest professional athlete who has come forward to publically apologize for his or her unethical actions. You may need to be *invisible*, per se, as some companies do not want it known that their executives don't write their own presentations. As a speech writer, you must be thick-skinned and open to criticism, as your speech drafts will be reviewed and edited by several people prior to delivery.

The speech writer must pay close attention to details. This means fact-checking and proofreading. For example, one small mistake on the part of the speech writer could be disastrous for a CEO who, when providing the annual fiscal report to his board of directors, discovers that the

© Brian A Jackson/Shutterstock.com

numbers don't add up. Similarly, for the politician on the campaign trail, a story used to create emotional appeal that can't be verified could permanently damage your candidate's credibility.

THE PROCESS

Research

You may write for someone with whom you've had very little contact, so you need to learn as much about the speaking style of your boss or client and collect material that you think would sound like the person you write for. If the person you write for makes use of particular phrases, then the speech should echo the speaker's style. For example, if the speaker makes use of colloquialisms, like President Barack Obama's use of "folks," you will want to make sure to include

© Matt Antonino/Shutterstock.com

that word. You want to have a good sense of the language that makes the speaker sound authentic and credible. You should collect anecdotes and stories from the speaker so the presentation that you write sounds authentic to that particular speaker. This means you must meet with the speaker and pay attention to her personality and tone. If you can, try to read past presentations the speaker has given to get an even better idea of the speaker's style. Research your speaker.

While we recognize how important it is for you to understand the speaker, it is equally important for you to know the audience that will be receiving the message. Again, research is the key. You want to find out as much as possible about the audience. This includes the audience's views on the particular topic, whether the audience has the potential to be hostile, if there are cultural considerations that the speaker will need to keep in mind, and even the age group of the particular audience. Now it is time to do your research.

Research may involve interviewing the speaker, interviewing your boss' staff, reviewing financial reports, interviewing subject matter experts, and finding out as much as you can about the event itself.

Preparing the Presentation

You are asked to write a speech for your boss. As the speech writer, it is your responsibility to research and accurately convey the essence of what the speaker wants to say. Define one clear message. If you could have only one sentence to say to the audience, what would that one message be? Everything else you say should support that one message. Once you know your

© wavebreakmedia/Shutterstock.com

message and you have done your research, it is time to make an outline. Recall the importance of outlining that we stressed in Chapter 1. Outlining helps you shape your ideas. The outline becomes the building blocks for the presentation and provides logical development of the material. The outline can also help you keep your material flexible. Once you have completely developed the outline, you can start writing the manuscript or talking points for the speaker. Some speakers prefer talking points while others want the entire word-for-word manuscript. Of course, the situation and formality of the occasion will dictate that more than anything. For example, if a corporate spokesperson is speaking on camera with a teleprompter, it is advantageous for the speaker to have the entire script.

Once you have developed a draft of the presentation that you are satisfied with, send the draft to the speaker and any others who may have a say in its final outcome. The speaker may meet with you personally, or she may send comments and changes electronically. You may end up doing several drafts before the presentation is finalized.

There will be times when the speaker will also need to be prepared to respond to questions or comments from the audience, so you should also anticipate some of these and have some responses ready for the speaker. These responses should be reviewed and rehearsed by the speaker. We will talk more about rehearsal in the next section on stagecraft and executive coaching.

STAGECRAFT AND EXECUTIVE COACHING

Rehearsal

Many speech writers double as the executive speaking coach for their bosses or clients. The coach needs to inform the speaker about the physical arrangements of the presentation so that they can rehearse under conditions that are as similar as possible to the actual speaking situation. This means sound, light, visuals, and nonverbal delivery practice. In other words, if the speaker is going to be in a very large auditorium, it is unlikely that the audience will be able to see gestures. Conversely, if the presentation is televised, the camera will be able to pick up even the slightest nervous tendency. The speaker must rehearse the presentation out loud. Reading a manuscript, versus speaking it out loud, can have very different results. This is how you determine where you need to make modifications or eliminate awkward words and phrases. Furthermore, you will get a sense of what is impactful in the presentation and what is simply extraneous filler. Edit, trim,

© Dima Groshev/Shutterstock.com

or add something additional to clarify a point. Perhaps that story that you thought was going to amplify a point doesn't really sound sincere when the speaker tells it. As a coach, you will recommend modifications. You might suggest ways to change the delivery to make it seem more genuine, you may suggest a different story, or you may do away with it all together.

Stagecraft

In addition to working with the speaker on his or her spoken words, we would be remiss if we didn't also encourage careful planning with stagecraft. Stagecraft encompasses everything about the speaker's space: proximity to audience, the lighting, seating arrangement, location of projector and screen,

© Maxim Tarasyugin/Shutterstock.com

podium or lectern, and whether there will be a microphone. Stagecraft should also take into consideration the speaker's dress and nonverbal elements of her delivery. The executive speech coach's job is to prepare the speaker for all of the physical and visual elements surrounding the presentation, in addition to the spoken word.

If your speaker is scheduled to speak in a large room, it is likely that she will not only have a lectern, but she will have a microphone as well. Practicing with both helps ensure a successful delivery. The speaker will have to really emphasize her gestures in order for them to be seen. How will the speaker use her notes with a lectern? Again, planned rehearsals eliminate last-minute concerns with details. You also do not want to worry about amplification. Make sure the speaker keeps the microphone close to her mouth so she can be heard. You do not want your speaker to be the one asking, "Can everyone hear me?"

The speaker should also rehearse with her visuals. Nothing can decrease the speaker's credibility more than fumbling with equipment in front of the audience when she is supposed to be speaking. Rehearse with visuals so as to ensure that the speaker will fit the presentation within the allotted timeframe. This is especially important if there are several speakers, as we emphasized in Chapter 5.

As an executive coach, it is your responsibility to make sure your speaker sounds good and looks good. We've all heard the importance of dressing for success. This is crucial in public speaking. A good rule of thumb is to dress one notch above your audience. For example, if your Human Resources Director has gathered automobile assemblers in an auditorium to inform them of changes in their medical plan, the Human Resources person would probably wear nice slacks and a collared shirt rather than a formal

© Russell Shively/Shutterstock.com

suit. Similarly, when the President speaks to locals in their hometown during a weather-related disaster, you will likely see him in slacks and a collared shirt with his sleeves rolled up. For more formal gatherings, men should wear a suit and tie and women should wear a suit or a dress. If your speaker is going to be televised, he should be advised to wear bold, solid colors so he does not look washed out. Additionally, distracting or large personal adornments, such as oversized jewelry, should be avoided.

On the day of the actual presentation, the speaker should check the set-up of the room to make sure the speaker, the visuals, and the stage can be seen from every seat. The equipment should be checked and cued up so the speaker's use of visuals will be seamless. This kind of preparation also gives the speaker one less thing to worry about.

The goal is to have the speaker step up in front of the audience with confidence, making sure his message is congruent with his nonverbal messages. If the speaker claims to be passionate about his topic, his body language had better reinforce the claim. Facial expressions, gestures, posture and vocal emphasis are key to ensuring congruity. Smile, if smiling is appropriate to the topic. Nothing builds rapport with an audience better than a smile.

If it is at all possible, we recommend having the executive speech coach in attendance for the speaker's presentations. This way the coach can help reinforce what has gone well, as well as offer tips for improvement after the presentation. The speech coach can also watch for the audience's reaction to the presentation. The coach might pick up on things that the speaker doesn't. Whether the coach notices audience members nodding heads in agreement with the speaker, spontaneously applauding after a particularly powerful statement, or laughing at appropriate times, she can report back to the speaker and reinforce the techniques that the speaker used well. Conversely, if the coach can pinpoint where the audience

© antb/Shutterstock.com

started to check their phones, watches, or look bored, she can help the speaker restructure or refocus a particular message to maintain audience engagement.

Whether you are writing a speech for someone else or coaching a CEO before a presentation, careful preparation and rehearsal greatly increases the chances of a well-received presentation. Speakers can benefit from working with a speaking coach both before and after a presentation. In public relations, image is everything. We want you or your speaker to project the best possible image in any speaking situation.

In this chapter we discussed your role as executive speech writer and coach. We also addressed those all-important considerations related to effective stagecraft. As a public relations professional, you will not only write speeches for yourself but will also be tasked with writing for, and coaching, someone else who serves as spokesperson for the organization. By now you should feel confident in your ability to do both. In the next chapter we look closely at both traditional media considerations and social media considerations in speech writing for public relations professionals.

© eurobanks/Shutterstock.com

Have you ever said something to someone and it was misinterpreted by that person? This is known in the profession as *intent versus impact*. For example, a large chemical company has had a significant chemical spill at one of its plants that has contaminated the local water supply and protected marshlands. In the initial press conference the CEO, with all good intentions, steps up to the microphone and explains the technical malfunction that caused the spill. She laments the cost of lost revenue to the organization. Her <u>intent</u> was to present the facts to assuage the media and community's fears and anger. Instead, the <u>impact</u> of the message on the community members was a lack of compassion and care on the part of the organization as it relates to the welfare of the community and wildlife. Rather than mitigating hostile public opinion, this well-intentioned CEO instead fanned the flames of community outrage. As such, it is absolutely essential to know your audience and have an understanding of what <u>meaning</u> your message will convey to that particular audience under those particular circumstances. Otherwise, a well-intended message could actually do more harm than good. It is your job as the public relations speech writer and executive coach to ensure your executive has that awareness and sensitivity.

REVIEW TERMS AND CONCEPTS

- ✓ Speech writer's role
- ✓ Research
- ✓ Preparing the presentation
- ✓ Rehearsal
- ✓ Stagecraft
- ✓ Executive coaching

APPLICATION IN ACTION

1. As a public relations professional, you will not only write speeches for yourself but will also be tasked with writing for, and coaching, someone else who serves as spokesperson for the organization.

2. Persuasion is at the heart of most public relations messages. Create a persuasive speech on behalf of a social cause to be delivered by a classmate.

© Oilyy/Shutterstock.com

I. Purpose
   A. The primary purpose of a speech on behalf of a social cause is to persuade the audience to adopt the speaker's and/or organization's point of view.

II. Objectives
   A. Prepare a persuasive speech on behalf of a social cause in a 2- to 3-page outline for a classmate following the format of the template and guidelines of the rubric located at the end of this chapter.
   B. Deliver a 6- to 7-minute speech on behalf of a social cause from an outline created by a classmate using an electronic visual aid.
   C. Observe speeches on behalf of a social cause given by other members of the class.
   D. Practice researching, writing, organizing and speaking skills.
   E. Practice a type of speech you may use later in your professional career (practical application).

III. Instructions
   A. You are the public relations spokesperson for a social cause of your choice.
   B. Your presentation must advocate on behalf of a social cause that you have selected from a list provided by your instructor. Topics must be pre-approved by your instructor to avoid redundancy.
   C. The presentation should contain both logical and emotional appeal.
   D. Create an outline (bibliography included) based on the information you will present. **Bring a typed copy of your outline as well as the rubric to class** with your name on it to give to the instructor just prior to presenting your speech.

SPEECH OUTLINE TEMPLATE

Instructions. You will use this template to create the draft of your speech outline.
   1. Remove these two pages from your textbook.
   2. Complete each section using a pencil (this will allow you to easily make changes).
   3. Exchange your completed draft with your speech coach for feedback.
   4. Submit your edited draft to your instructor on the assigned date.

Specific Purpose:

_____

_____

Thesis Statement:

_____

_____

_____

Introduction

     I.   *Attention-getting material:*

     II.   *Establish credibility:*

     III.   *Preview/thematic statement:*

     [Transition: _____.]

Body

     I.   _____
           A.
           B.
           C.

     [Transition: _____.]

(*Body continued*)
    II. _____
            A.
            B.
            C.

            [Transition: _____.]

    III. _____
            A.
            B.
            C.

            [Transition: _____.]

    IV. _____
            A.
            B.
            C.

            [Transition: _____.]

Conclusion

    I.   *Summary Statement:*

    II.   *Concluding Remarks:*

Bibliography

1.
2.
3.

PERSUASIVE SPEECH EVALUATION RUBRIC

NAME _____	
CONTENT	**DELIVERY**
INTRODUCTION (10 POINTS) • Opening statement that <u>doesn't announce topic</u> (Attention getter) • Establishes credibility • Previews the speech • Thesis Statement	**EYE CONTACT** (10 POINTS) • Directness • Randomness
BODY (10 POINTS) • 2- to 3-page typewritten outline following the three-level, full-sentence format (no paragraphs), numbering, and general appearance in the textbook • Contains evidence of solid research • Contains logical and emotional appeal • Major points of the speech are linked with <u>transitions</u>	**VOICE & MOVEMENT** (5 POINTS) • Projection • Minimal Vocalized Pauses • Posture • Gestures
CONCLUSION (5 POINTS) • Summarizes the main points of the speech • Ends with a quotation, story, or ties back to opening sentence ("clincher")	**TIME** (10 POINTS) • Conformed to 6- to 7-minute time limit
VISUAL AID (10 POINTS) • Handling of Aid • Appearance	
TIME: GRADE:	

Coaching for Persuasive Speech

Assignment: Remove this page from your text and bring to class on the day that your speaking partner presents their speech. During the presentation, take notes based on the questions provided below. Then, write a one- to two-page critique discussing your answers to those questions as you assess your speaking partner. This should be written in paragraph form.

1. How convincing was the speaker in advocating the cause?

2. "How effective was the speaker's emotional appeal? Explain."**

3. What was included to project speaker enthusiasm? Dramatic flair? Colorful word choice?

4. "Comment on the speaker's voice, gestures, and facial expressions? Were they used appropriately to engage the audience? Was the voice modulated in pitch and volume?"**

Credits:

**Toastmasters *Advanced Communication Series Public Relations*

Speaking to the Media

© Pavel L Photo and Video/Shutterstock.com

Objectives

At the completion of this chapter you should be able to:

- ✓ Explain the importance of the relationship between public relations and the media.

- ✓ Describe various situations in which public relations professionals interact with the media.

- ✓ Understand appropriate and inappropriate communication behaviors and actions when dealing with the media.

- ✓ Demonstrate your understanding of media considerations through the delivery of a crisis response speech to an audience that will ask questions.

So far in this book we have discussed preparing your speech and visual aids, audience and presenter considerations, and different kinds of speeches you can expect as a public relations speech writer and presenter. This chapter deals with a specific audience: the media.

TRADITIONAL MEDIA CONSIDERATIONS

You may have heard of some instances where public relations professionals fear or distrust the media. We believe that it is immensely important for the public relations professional to recognize that the media professional, like the public relations professional, has a

© wellphoto/Shutterstock.com

job to do. Both professions, the media and public relations, need each other in order to be successful in today's business environment. And while the relationship between public relations and the media is often characterized as contentious, it doesn't have to be. The cause, more often than not, is a lack of understanding by the public relations professional of the challenges facing journalists in an evolving media landscape. In reality, today's media environment is the best it has ever been for public relations professionals. They can quickly and easily get their message or their client's/organization's story broadcast, in print or on the web.

It is to your benefit as the public relations speech writer to establish a good relationship with your local media contacts. The onus is on you to make that first gesture. That first outreach might consist of inviting your media contact for a cup of coffee. This manner of initial contact is preferred instead of lunch (or dinner) in order to keep the introductory meeting short, out of respect for the journalist's time. Subsequent meetings could involve a lengthier scenario, such as lunch.

The first step in creating a harmonious relationship with the media is for the public relations professional to understand and empathize with the challenges that today's print and broadcast journalists face. This includes shrinking newsrooms, fewer reporters and more work, and a very competitive 24/7 news cycle.

© Albert H. Teich/Shutterstock.com

The second step is for you to recognize that the broadcast and print journalism professions aren't going away, they are simply changing. For example, journalists have become more research-oriented. This means they are increasingly reliant on obtaining information and stories about organizations from the Internet as a matter of efficiency. Also, press releases posted to the website or emailed to a media contact are more apt to be published verbatim as news stories, rather than being rewritten, which has been the practice in the past. For instance, there have been cases where journalists have printed verbatim, as a story, a press release posted on an organization's website without the organization's knowledge.

In light of this context, public relations professionals must be available to be contacted by the media 24 hours a day, seven days a week. A common complaint from reporters is that their public relations contact will send them something, but is not available after the end of normal business hours for clarifications or questions the reporter may have. This could mean the loss of a crucial publicity opportunity for that organization.

Further, public relations professionals must build trust with their media contacts and provide objective and open information about the organization. After all, the public relations profession prides itself on transparency and ethical conduct. Now let's look at some specific interactions between public relations and the media.

PRESS CONFERENCES

Press conferences are infrequent albeit very important events that are used to inform your publics through the media about happenings in your organization, ranging from events to breaking news. Not all situations require a press conference. Sometimes a one-on-one interview may be more appropriate, such as in the case of highly technical information.

© Pavel L Photo and Video/Shutterstock.com

Press conferences can be useful when a lot of media interest is expected. This way, as the spokesperson, you can provide one answer for many reporters, thereby keeping your message consistent. *Webster's New World Dictionary, Third College Edition* defines a press conference as "a collective interview granted to media personnel as by a celebrity or personage." The term *collective interview* is important because it means a group face-to-face setting that is interactive (as opposed to one-way). This is an important distinction, and differs from an organization simply making a public statement. A common complaint voiced by reporters is an organization's promise of a press conference that is, in reality, a spokesperson simply providing talking points and not allowing an opportunity for the media to ask questions. This sort of bait-and-switch tactic is disrespectful of the journalist's time.

161

A true press conference contains a statement from the organization <u>and</u> an opportunity for questions from the journalist audience. And while the public relations speech writer should do his best to satisfy the needs of the press in attendance, he must ensure the organization's spokesperson, either himself or another, represents the organization and conveys the message professionally and effectively.

Since you don't have an opportunity for a "do over" as you would have in creating a video for the organization's website, it is important to remember that press conferences are live. Therefore, you need to get it right the first time. Getting it right includes your attention to stagecraft (as we

© photographer/Shutterstock.com

discussed in Chapter 7), which is the environment where the press conference will take place. Approach this from a perspective of audience comfort and host image. Provide a room of sufficient size and adequate chairs for the media in attendance. The room should be large enough to accommodate journalists with cameras.

Make sure the location is relatively free of ambient noise, such as automobiles and aircraft. Recall the example in the Chapter 5 (Nonverbal Communication) in which the CEO of a major airline gave his first media briefing within minutes after one of its aircraft crash-landed in a New York river. The CEO's announcement was very well done; however, it was delivered outdoors next to an airport, and the noise of aircraft flying overhead made it difficult to hear his statement.

Ensure sufficient audiovisual support such as outlets, microphone, cords, lighting, etc.

Remember to test the sound system. In our experience, sound systems are often very fragile and almost always fail. The backdrop behind the speaker is equally important. The backdrop conveys a strong visual image so it must be professional, and not haphazard, in appearance. The backdrop might have your organization's name and logo on it to promote continuity in branding. Finally, pick a location that has adequate parking and access to the conference room.

Spokesperson Considerations

As an organizational spokesperson, it is important that you control the agenda of the press conference. This includes the timing of the event. For example, if you have a positive announcement to make, then you would want to schedule your press

© Brian A Jackson/Shutterstock.com

conference at 10 a.m. This ensures that your announcement is the lead on the 5 p.m. news and is also headlined the next day. Conversely, if you are in "damage control mode" in the midst of a crisis, schedule your press conference at 3 p.m. This gives reporters in attendance little time to do any research and thereby guarantees that the lead on the 5 p.m. news and the following morning's headline is confined to what you announced.

The focal point of any press conference is you or your spokesperson. It is important to remember as a spokesperson that 93 percent of your communication is nonverbal and only seven percent is verbal when it comes to being received by your audience. Body language matters. Also, likability of you, the spokesperson, is a significant factor in message reception and your audience will decide whether or not they like you within the first 15 seconds of your presentation. As such, you or your spokesperson need to be at the top of your game from the start—there is no "warm up."

You or your spokesperson should be experienced in the subject so that you can respond to reporter's questions after your initial statement. It is important that you or your spokesperson understand the role and needs of the reporters in attendance, understand the organization, understand the situation that has called for a press conference, and are able to credibly respond to questions posed by the reporters. Above all, treat all media with respect and strive to maintain a cool, calm and controlled demeanor. Audiences often remember impressions, not facts.

This leads us to the crafting of your message. Be very clear about your specific purpose or goals of your press conference. Remember that you must have something newsworthy to talk about. To avoid confusion or misunderstanding by the listener, do not introduce too much information. Also, your message must reach the average person, i.e., the reader or viewer who may be totally unfamiliar with the issue about which you are speaking. The way to avoid confusion and achieve this understanding is through the use of sound bites. Sound bites are the refinement of your message into short phrases that are easy to remember and provide succinct statements of your position.

> **Perception is Reality**
>
> You and your spokesperson's level of preparation are directly proportional to the audience's perceived professionalism of the organization. The more effort expended in rehearsal and stagecraft preparations, the more positive image the audience will have, which is especially important because audiences tend to equate professionalism with credibility. The more credibility you or your spokesperson have with the audience, the greater success you will have in conveying your message because the audience will be more receptive to your message.

Prepare your message using memorable and short sound bites so the only quotable material that you are giving reporters is that which amplifies your key message. In this vein, you should have three to four talking points that you consistently return to as necessary. Remember, what you say is likely to be quoted or replayed. Once you've condensed your message into solid sound bites and you have your facts and arguments lined up to support that message, you're ready to meet the media. Stay on message.

Delivery and dress are your next considerations in a successful press conference. When creating your speaker notes, use a large font size, such as 16 or 18 point, to make it readable from distance. Highlight key points in your speaker notes as necessary to guide your delivery. Speak slowly and clearly. Stick with your prepared text even if it means repeating yourself and avoid any unplanned remarks. Recall from Chapter 6 (Delivering the Presentation) the power of the pause. Always tell the truth and never speak off the record. As also mentioned in Chapter 6, keep your presentation within the published time limits of the event.

© R. Gino Santa Maria/Shutterstock.com

Your spokesperson's appearance is important because it helps to establish credibility. In this sense, always wear appropriate attire. Also, presume there will be broadcast television cameras in attendance. Therefore, to present a credible TV appearance, wear dark, solid-colored outfits and avoid stripes, checks or small patterns. Compliment these with a light-blue or pastel-colored shirt or blouse.

Reporters attending a press conference expect the opportunity to ask questions either during or following your planned remarks. Consequently, you need to anticipate and prepare responses. A characteristic of an effective press conference is anticipating the questions the press will ask. Journalists typically pose their questions along the lines of who, what, where, when, why, and how.

When responding to questions from reporters we suggest doing so in the following manner. First, listen closely to the question. Second, repeat the question aloud. This ensures that everyone in the audience understands the question and gives you time to think about your response. Third, pause for a few seconds before responding. This gives you additional time to think about the question and signals to the reporter and audience that you are giving the question serious consideration. Finally, answer the question directly. This means looking directly at the reporter who posed the question and giving a succinct answer.

© MilanMarkovic78/Shutterstock.com

When responding to questions, always answer the questions asked, no more and no less. Keep your answers simple and concise. If you don't know the answer to a reporter's question, say that you don't know the answer or that you will check into it and get back to the reporter. Never say "no comment" because that creates an assumption of guilt or at least that you are hiding information. Instead, tell the questioner the reason why you can't comment, such as "it's premature to say." By all means, remain confident and in control.

Social Media Considerations

Now let's take a look at the social media communication channel as a means of conveying our message to the media. In today's "point-and-click" society there is an expectation that everything will be posted to some form of social media. A common practice is for organizations to video their press conferences, then post them to their website.

As mentioned earlier in this chapter, the media has become increasingly reliant on the Internet for finding information and stories about organizations. So, another way the organization can get their message out, albeit non-interactive, is to create a video of the CEO making a statement, then posting it to the

© Quka/Shutterstock.com

organization's website and YouTube. The upside to this method is that you have plenty of opportunities for retakes because it isn't live. The downside is that there is no opportunity for questions to be posed by the audience, which, depending on the circumstances, can affect the credibility of the presentation. However, as is the case in a live press conference, the appearance of the speaker and all aspects of delivery are critically important. The background is an important stagecraft consideration because this is all that the viewer will see in the video. Remember, this is an opportunity to reinforce the brand. Position the logo near the speaker. Remind the speaker that this is a set and not to wander outside of the set.

In this final chapter we talked about various encounters between public relations professionals and the media in a public speaking context. By now you should feel confident in creating and delivering presentations for yourself and others in a variety of public speaking contexts in the public relations profession.

Coach's Corner: The Devil is in the Details

When preparing for a live press conference, it is essential to have a checklist to ensure that all the details are covered. Often these events are held in stressful contexts, such as communicating details about a crisis. In these situations, it is difficult to keep all of the logistical details in our head. For example, ensuring things like adequate seating for the audience, a functional sound system, A/V system checks, and even a bottle of water at the podium for the speaker, are essential for a professionally-conducted event.

© eurobanks/Shutterstock.com

REVIEW TERMS AND CONCEPTS

- ✓ Traditional media considerations

- ✓ Press conferences

- ✓ Talking points

- ✓ Sound bites

- ✓ Appearance considerations

- ✓ Handling questions

- ✓ Social media considerations

APPLICATION IN ACTION

1. Public relations professionals must build trust with their media contacts and provide objective and open information about the organization.

2. Press conferences are infrequent events that are used to inform your publics through the media about happenings in your organization, ranging from events to breaking news occurrences, such as an organizational crisis. A crisis response speech is a

© Oilyy/Shutterstock.com

public relations strategy intended to demonstrate to your audience that the organization is aware of the situation, cares, and is doing what it is supposed to be doing to resolve the situation. Create and deliver a crisis response speech about a current or past public relations crisis and respond to audience questions.

I. Purpose
   A. The primary purpose of a crisis response speech is to assure your publics that the organization is aware of the situation, cares, and is doing what it is supposed to be doing to resolve the situation.

II. Objectives
   A. Prepare a crisis response speech in a 2- to 3-page outline following the format of the template and guidelines of the rubric located at the end of this chapter.
   B. Deliver a 4- to 5-minute crisis response speech from an outline followed by a two minute question and answer session from the audience.
   C. Observe crisis response speeches given by other members of the class.
   D. Practice researching, writing, organizing and speaking skills.
   E. Practice a type of speech you may use later in your professional career (practical application).

III. Instructions
   A. You are the public relations spokesperson for a company or celebrity of your choice that is either currently experiencing a crisis or has experienced a crisis in the past (which would be presented as if occurring today).

B. In addition to the crisis response considerations discussed above, your presentation must address what went wrong, how it will be fixed, and what will be done to ensure it won't happen again.

C. Your response should not repeat what has already been published about the crisis but instead be your original work.

D. Respond to audience questions by practicing the question response techniques discussed in the chapter.

E. Create an outline (bibliography included) based on the information you will present. **<u>Bring a typed copy of your outline as well as the rubric to class</u>** with your name on it to give to the instructor just prior to presenting your speech.

SPEECH OUTLINE TEMPLATE

Instructions. You will use this template to create the draft of your speech outline.
   1. Remove these two pages from your textbook.
   2. Complete each section using a pencil (this will allow you to easily make changes).
   3. Exchange your completed draft with your speech coach for feedback.
   4. Submit your edited draft to your instructor on the assigned date.

Specific Purpose:

_____

_____

Thesis Statement:

_____

_____

_____

Introduction
   I.   *Attention-getting material:*

   II.   *Establish credibility:*

   III.   *Preview/thematic statement:*

         [Transition: _____.]

Body

   I.   _____
         A.
         B.
         C.

         [Transition: _____.]

(Body continued)

II. _____
    A.
    B.
    C.

    [Transition: _____.]

III. _____
    A.
    B.
    C.

    [Transition: _____.]

IV. _____
    A.
    B.
    C.

    [Transition: _____ .]

Conclusion
I.   *Summary Statement:*

II.   *Concluding Remarks:*

Bibliography

1.
2.
3.

CRISIS RESPONSE SPEECH EVALUATION RUBRIC

CONTENT		DELIVERY
NAME _____		
CONTENT		**DELIVERY**
INTRODUCTION (10 POINTS) • Opening statement that <u>doesn't</u> <u>announce topic</u> (Attention getter) • Establishes credibility • Previews the speech • Thesis Statement		**EYE CONTACT** (10 POINTS) • Directness • Randomness
BODY (10 POINTS) • 2- to 3-page typewritten outline following the three-level, full-sentence format (no paragraphs), numbering, and general appearance in the textbook • Contains evidence of solid research • Demonstrates care and addresses what went wrong, how it will be fixed, and what will be done to ensure it won't happen again • Major points of the speech are linked with <u>transitions</u>		**VOICE & MOVEMENT** (5 POINTS) • Projection • Minimal Vocalized Pauses • Posture • Gestures
CONCLUSION (5 POINTS) • Summarizes the main points of the speech • Ends with a quotation, story, or ties back to opening sentence ("clincher")		**TIME** (10 POINTS) • Conformed to 4- to 5-minute time limit
VISUAL AID (10 POINTS) • Handling of Aid • Appearance		
TIME:	GRADE:	

Coaching for Informative Speech

Assignment: Remove this page from your text and bring to class on the day that your speaking partner presents their speech. During the presentation, take notes based on the questions provided below. Then, write a one- to two-page critique discussing your answers to those questions as you assess your speaking partner. This should be written in paragraph form.

1. How well did the speaker describe their crisis response, including what went wrong, how it will be fixed, and what will be done to ensure it won't happen again?

2. How effective was the speaker's use of visuals? Explain.

3. How well did the speaker respond to audience questions? Discuss their effectiveness in terms of the question response techniques described in the chapter.

4. "Comment on the speaker's voice, gestures, and facial expressions? Were they used appropriately to engage the audience? Was the voice modulated in pitch and volume?"**

5. Based on all of the speeches you've seen the speaker give this semester, comment on noticeable improvements.

Credits:

**Toastmasters *Advanced Communication Series Public Relations*

CPSIA information can be obtained
at www.ICGtesting.com
Printed in the USA
LVHW011030061219
639623LV00001BA/3/P

9 781465 266545